CW00590422

# CRIME COMPONENTS

## ARIZONA HOMICIDE FILES BOOK 1

## RENA WINTERS

Copyright (C) 2021 Rena Winters

Layout design and Copyright (C) 2021 by Next Chapter

Published 2021 by Next Chapter

Edited by Icarus O'Brien-Scheffer

Cover art by CoverMint

This book is a work of fiction. Names, characters, places, and incidents are the product of the author's imagination or are used fictitiously. Any resemblance to actual events, locales, or persons, living or dead, is purely coincidental. Although a work of fiction, it is based on actual homicide events in the State of Arizona.

All rights reserved. No part of this book may be reproduced or transmitted in any form or by any means, electronic or mechanical, including photocopying, recording, or by any information storage and retrieval system, without the author's permission.

# PREFACE

Early in Gene McLain's career as an investigative reporter, there were no computers, internet, cell phones, boom boxes, seat belts, air bags, VHS, CD's, DVD's, or any of the technology we take for granted today.

There was no Miranda-Escobeda law. When you were arrested, police could get confessions any way they wanted. Also, there was no known way of matching DNA.

There was no "America's Most Wanted" or "CSI".

Television was new and the nation was amazed at black and white pictures. The passenger jets we fly in today were just a dream on a drawing board.

We did have crime, and that's what this is all about: the world of homicide, Gene McLain's world. He not only wrote award winning stories about crimes, he *solved* them.

# PROLOGUE

THE APRIL EVENING IS IN ITS FINAL MINUTES BEFORE SUNSET. The cloud formations over the mountains south of Phoenix, Arizona are fantastic. Big and soft, with the rays of the setting sun making colored patterns against the white background.

The slopes are covered with cactus in full bloom and the soft breezes play through the mesquite and chaparral, whispering that, in a few hours, Easter will arrive.

For a while, the only sounds are those of nature. At first faint, then growing louder, voices mingle with, then override, the natural sounds of the area. The first voice is soft, but speaks with great urgency.

"I can't do this. The wire's cutting into his wrists."

"I'm tired of your complaining," a forceful voice replies. "Take another full wrap around his wrists, then bend it. That's it. You've got it. Now, down on your knees, Mama's boy. Get your hands behind your back. Don't try anything funny, or I'll kill you before you can even start to turn around."

The soft voice let out a sob. "Please, don't hurt us. We promise not to identify you. Please, my mother needs me. She's an invalid and I take care of her. Please, for her sake."

A husky voice mixed with tears and emotion enters the conversation.

"Please, fella', we didn't do anything to you. Please listen to me. I want to live. I want to live! Please, Please!"

The owner of that husky voice breaks into a long burst of crying. The soft voice interjects.

"Look, you have your whole life in front of you. Don't hurt us. If you do, the law will track you down and ..."

The forceful voice breaks into laughter. "You're wrong, pal. There won't be any law after me. You see, there's no motive.

This is the perfect crime. You know, you're lucky. Your part in this will make you famous in legal history. You'll be remembered as a key part of the perfect crime."

There is a rustling in the underbrush and the husky voice screams. "Get that gun away from my head! I want to live, damn it. Don't you understand? I want to live—"

The explosion of a .45 caliber automatic destroys the solitude of the mountains as the air momentarily fills with a gory display of blood, brains, and shattered bone.

When the echoes of the gunfire subside, the soft voice cries out in halted speech, "Mother, I'm so sorry, and Ruth, I love you with all my heart. The Lord is my shepherd. He makes—"

The .45 explodes. Once again blood, flesh, and bone fill the desert air. The echo of the shot bounces off the canyon walls. Then, it's silent. From afar the birds resume their singing, and the soft breezes continue to whisper.

Feet grind into the rocks. A car door opens and shuts. The engine turns over and is gunned. The air is filled with sand and gravel as the wheels spin. The car rockets away. The sound of the powerful engine grows fainter and fainter, until it is gone.

Dark shadows fall over the walls of the canyon as the sun sets. The moment before it slips behind the mountain, its rays strike the white of the clouds, creating a palette of colors. In the final seconds before vanishing, a blood red ray illuminates the bodies of two men in business suits laying face down in a shallow arroyo. Their hands are wired behind them. The backs of their heads have been destroyed.

Here in this lonely place where only the dead kept watch, and an act had been committed that later sets in motion a crime story like no other.

But, for now, the canyon is dark. Across the mountains, the lights of the city twinkle. Easter is just hours away. Soon, many lives will change by what has happened on this beautiful April evening.

# CHAPTER ONE

SOME KIDS GROW UP WANTING TO BE A FIREMAN, MOVIE STAR, mob boss, or President of the United States. I never wanted to be anything but a homicide reporter. I got my wish.

I wake up late this morning, which is highly unusual for me: I'm always an early riser. I never hear my wife Blondie leave the bed, dress for work, or feed the kids and get them off for school.

Last night, I was in Florence Junction covering the execution of the Gonzales brothers, a couple of young punks who pulled off several vicious murders. I went down early because there was going to be a picnic. The state of Arizona is very liberal when it comes to last visits by relatives on execution day. They give the families two or three hours together in a private room where they can touch, kiss, and embrace. When I spoke to Warden Franks about the upcoming executions, he told me he had a problem. The Gonzales family is a large one and they wanted to have a picnic to send the brothers off to a different world.

Frank Thomas is one tough guy. You wouldn't want to meet him in a dark alley, because he's the one who would come out of any fight. He likes to boast that he runs the toughest prison in the USA next to Leavenworth and Atlanta. He would be the last person to ever coddle a prisoner. He assumes they've been sent to "The Big House on The Gila," as the cons refer to this place of hell that stands on the banks of the Gila River, for punishment and not to join the country club. There's no television and only a few model cons are allowed to have radios. You'll find no exercise equipment in the sun baked exercise yard that has no trees. Exercise means you walk around and around in circles. Otherwise, you work or you're locked up. For Frank to even consider giving the Gonzales clan someplace for a picnic was almost unthinkable.

The only room that can be controlled that's large enough for the Gonzales clan is the "death" house. When I arrive with my Speed Graphic in hand for a couple of photos, I find that the ladies have spread white table cloths on the floor all along the front of the gas chamber, and have set out baskets of delicious Mexican food. They ask me to join them and I do. The picnic lasts until two hours prior to execution, when the family members say their tearful farewells. The young brothers deserve to die, but to their family they are sons, brothers and husbands.

The executions go off on schedule. Like ninety-nine percent of so-called tough guys, there is a lot of blubbering and tears. The good Padre tries to assure them that God will hear their story, and they might be granted forgiveness. The youngest brother collapses at the door to the chamber and has to be carried in. At last, sitting side by side, they are strapped in place and the door is locked. The Warden drops the cyanide pellets and their heads snap up when the first wisp of smoke brings the smell of peaches, which is the fragrance of lethal gas coming from the pellets. It's over quickly. The police, sheriffs, and a couple of out-of-state reporters file out.

I have a cup of coffee and a piece of pie with a friend who has come over to cover the execution for the *Los Angeles Examiner*. We start swapping old newspaper stories and it is later than I had planned when I start home. It's raining. This is no drizzle but a heavy spring rain and the going is slow. Blondie and the kids are asleep when I arrive and slip into bed.

Now soft streams of sunlight filter through the blinds that cover the open windows. It's a beautiful day and the breezes are soft and warm.

The Gonzales story is history and I'm anxious to get to my next assignment. As I drive into downtown Phoenix I can see that the snowbirds are packing up their golf equipment and getting ready to head east. We'll be seeing them come next October, when they'll flock to "The Valley of the Sun."

I find a parking spot behind the Maricopa County Court House. This is my home away from home. Inside, you'll find the Phoenix Police Department, Maricopa County Sheriff's Office, the jail, courtrooms, and the offices of the District Attorney, his staff, plus the judges chambers.

My target is the office of Chief Deputy Harry Morse, in charge of the Phoenix Police Department Missing Person's Division. I can tell by the way he squirms around that he's ready to go off duty. He's winding up some small talk with a couple of uniformed officers, Phil Rivera and Jimmy Lynch. Rivera spots me first and eyeballs my Hawaiian print shirt which I'm wearing tails-out over grey slacks.

"Look who we have here. I didn't think we'd be graced with your royal presence after winning another story of the year award."

Jimmy Lynch pats the left side of my shirt where I have the .38 clipped onto my belt.

"When you gonna' use that .38, McLain, and bring in one of those big, bad criminals?"

Rivera gives me no time to reply. "You're wrong, Jimmy. There's no time to have shoot-outs with criminals. Didn't you see the morning paper? He's too busy having dinner with the Gonzales Brothers."

I have to laugh at this kind of chatter.

"Okay, fellas, knock it off. The power of the press is here to get the real story."

Deputy Morse gets into the act. "I don't know about the power of the press. We had a fellow here today who calls himself a TV reporter. He came over from KPHO."

"Yeah," Lynch chimes in, "he told Harry that television has come to Arizona, and the newspapers are all washed up."

"You guys are too much. I'll let you know when the newspapers are out of business. Right now I want to find out about a missing person's story that, according to a hot rumor, was brought here earlier."

Morse punches off the lights in his office and moves into the hall before he answers. "There's no Missing Person's Report. Nothing at all to that rumor you heard. Didn't even take a complaint. There are no missing persons, just a couple of car salesmen off on a wild weekend in Mexico. Look Gene, if anything does turn up on this story I'll assign Blondie to the case, but there is no case."

The mention of Blondie sends Rivera and Lynch into gales of laughter. Rivera steps in front of Morse, tears streaming from his eyes.

"I like that Inspector. Give the case to Blondie."

This gets my quick reply. "Rivera, what are you talking about?"

Lynch grabs my arm.

"Blondie, you do remember your wife don't you? Tell me, McLain, how did a guy with a mug like yours ever convince that beautiful doll to marry you?"

I turn and walk down the corridor but shoot back over my shoulder, "Just good old Irish charm fellas, just good old Irish charm."

# CHAPTER TWO

I MAKE MY WAY OUT OF THE COURTHOUSE AND ACROSS THE street to my favorite coffee shop, the Legal Eagle. The Eagle, which serves the people working at the courthouse, is owned by a vivacious lady named Mary Olive Devlin, who's just a few years removed from her home in Dublin, Ireland.

I spot Blondie through the big plate glass window. All 5'4" of her, looking like a young Lana Turner. She's reading the newspaper. I have to stop for a second and murmur a prayer of thanks that I'm the lucky guy who married this lovely lady. She's dressed in her summer uniform: navy blue linen skirt and a crisp white, short-sleeved shirt.

As I enter, the milk and honey voice of Teresa Brewer comes from the radio behind the counter singing her hit, "Music, Music, Music." I hum a couple of lines along with her until John Mahoney, a well-known criminal attorney, says "Hello." We make small talk for a couple of seconds, then I move back to where my beautiful bride waits.

"How's my best girl?"

She gives me that million dollar smile that Hollywood would give a sack of gold to capture. "Your *only* girl is just fine. I ordered for you. Now, what's new?"

"Nothing I can put my finger on, but I have the feeling that something off the wall is going on with a supposed missing person's case that Morse tells me is 'not a case.'"

Blondie had happened to be in Harry's office when the woman came in. "I would say she's in her late fifties, nicely dressed, well-educated and level-headed. She wanted to file a missing persons report on a man who's a salesman at the Acme Auto Agency. Harry as good as told her that the man was on an extended drunk in Mexico, and not to worry. The kicker is that a second salesman who works for Acme is also missing."

This jolts me with that old feeling that homicide reporters like to refer to as their gut instinct. "Honey, something tells me I better go out to the Acme Auto Agency and check this out."

"Okay Gene, if you really think it's important, go ahead. I have to get home and take care of the boys. Mom is going over to the Martin's for dinner and I don't want to make her late. By the way, as I recall, you and I have some plans to spend quality time alone together this evening."

Blondie slides out of the booth and pulls her black, leather bag off the seat. She checks its interior to be certain her badge, gun, and ID are in place, then settles the strap over her left shoulder. She gives me a good look and plants a kiss on my cheek.

"Just don't take all night. I'll wait for you."

As Blondie makes her exit, every male eye in the joint watches the fluid hip movement under her skirt. You know, the cops are right when they wonder how a 5'8" guy like me, with a mug that came straight out of Ireland, ever got such a beautiful wife. They don't know that we were childhood sweethearts. I guess the man upstairs puts the right people together to make a perfect marriage.

I finish my snack, pay my bill, and move out of The Eagle into the soft desert night. I'm amazed how close the stars seem to be, up in the black velvet sky. I find my car on the lot and head out from Van Buren Street toward the Acme Auto Agency.

# CHAPTER THREE

OF ALL THE ESTABLISHMENTS ON VAN BUREN STREET, KNOWN to the locals as Auto Row, none are more magnificent than the Acme Auto Agency. Brand-new, highly polished Fords fill the three plate glass windows. I admire the layout for a few seconds before pushing through the glass doors and into what seems to be a deserted showroom.

Soft music plays as I wander down the hall bordering the sales offices. The maroon carpeting is thick and very plush so, without notice, I come upon a gentleman with a full head of grey, neatly trimmed hair. He's wearing a dark blue blazer, red striped tie, a white shirt, and grey slacks. I can smell his expensive aftershave. He's engrossed in an in-depth story about the fall prospects for the Arizona State College football team. He almost goes into shock when I speak in his ear.

"You must be a 'Whizzer' White fan."

His eyes widen and he reaches somewhere to find a reply. "I sure am. Wilford 'Whizzer' White is the best running back in the nation, and this is the year the Sun Devils are going to a major bowl."

"You'll get no argument from me on that subject. I think Arizona State College will take the Border Conference Championship and be playing in the big time come New Year's day."

The gentleman puts down his paper, stands, and we shake hands.

"Sorry, I get carried away with Sun Devil football. My name is Bill Broaddus and I'm the owner. Can I show you some of our great new cars?"

I could use something to replace my battered heap, but I give Mr. Broaddus the facts of life. "I'd love to own one of your new models, but it's not in my budget this year. I'm Gene McLain of the *Arizona Reporter*, and I'd like to know something about a couple of your salesmen that I understand are missing."

Broaddus clears his throat and starts to ramble. "It's kind of a funny thing. Early last Saturday, the Saturday before Easter, a young guy came in. Good looking kid. Tall and slender with dark curly hair. It seems he has an old Ford at home that he's thinking of trading. He asked for a demonstration ride, so 'Big George' Williams, the salesman on duty, said 'fine, let's go.'"

The name George Williams rings a bell loud and clear. When Broaddus refers to 'Big George' Williams, I am ninety-nine percent sure I know who he's talking about. "Hold on a second. This 'Big George' Williams you mentioned, is this the same George Williams who was once a member of the Arizona Highway Patrol?"

"One and the same. All six feet four, two hundred and forty-five pounds of solid muscle. That's George, all right."

"If I were you, I wouldn't worry about George. He's one tough cookie."

Broaddus waves his arms to signal me to stop talking. "You don't understand. I would never worry a second about George. He goes on a jag about twice a year. These little 'vacations,' as he calls them, can run from a week to an entire month or more. Since he's on straight commission, it's no big deal. When George is here he sells twice as many cars as any other salesman."

"Okay, so what's the difference about George being gone this time?"

Broaddus's face flushes as he starts to twist and turn. "Mr. McLain, the problem is not George. The problem is Severson. Harold Severson is a top quality young man who's only been with us for two months."

"Mr. Broaddus, I don't quite follow you. How does Severson get into George William's act?"

"George was all ready to take the young client for a demo ride. Severson had just gone off duty and he asked George if he would drop him at his apartment while George and the client checked the car out. George said okay, and the client didn't mind, so Severson went back to his office, cleaned off his desk and announced he was ready. At 6:15, last Saturday evening, the three of them drove out of here with the car. That was a week ago. The car, the client, George and Severson have all vanished. My guess is that George and Severson dumped the client and after a couple of beers, George talked young Severson into going with him to enjoy the booze, the gambling, and the ladies that the lovely land south of the border has to offer."

Something doesn't fit. I run Broaddus' dialogue through my mind on fast forward. "Didn't you say the client didn't drive here in the car he wanted to trade?"

"That's right. Someone drove him in or he got a ride. Anyway, he left the old car at home."

"That's really different, if you want to talk about a trade. What car did George use to give the client a demo ride?"

Broaddus wipes the smile off his face, which turns stern. "That's what really ticks me off about this whole affair."

"How's that?"

"They took the only convertible I have in stock. A real beauty—apple red with a white top. I just hope it doesn't get scratched or dented while they are visiting the flesh pots. It's a beautiful piece of merchandise."

I let the tape in my mind make one more pass on the information that Broaddus has furnished. "Thanks, Mr. Broaddus. You've given me some things to think about."

The smile is back on his face. He looks the part of a successful businessman. Very fashionable and slender.

"Anytime that I can be of help, please feel free to call on me, McLain."

I start to move through the cars on the showroom floor, then stop and look back at Broaddus, who is standing where I left him.

"You know, Mr. Broaddus," I say to him, "you seem so certain that a spree in Mexico is the answer. Something inside me tells me this never happened."

I push through the glass doors out into the warmth. I look back. Broaddus hasn't moved. Instead, he looks as though my final words have hit him like a ton of bricks.

# CHAPTER FOUR

WHEN I GET HOME, BLONDIE IS GETTING THE KIDS READY FOR bed. Little Larry and Jerry rush out to see their dad and get a kiss. I find my dinner in the oven where my wife has kept it warm. I pour a cup of coffee then start on my food like a starving man. Blondie comes in wearing a pretty blue robe. She gets a cup and saucer from the cupboard, fills her cup, and joins me at the kitchen table.

I fill her in on my trip to Acme Auto and my meeting with the owner, Bill Broaddus.

"You know, Blondie, this guy is like everyone else that's involved so far. They all seem to think Williams and Severson are in Mexico on one of the sprees that George Williams is famous for."

Her blue eyes are sparkling and I know that something important is about to unfold.

"Well, I have a new twist for you. On the way home I realized I had left the gas bill and our mortgage payment on my desk, so I turned around and drove back to headquarters to get them. Coming down the stairs, I ran into the middle-aged woman who had tried to get Harry to make out a Missing Persons report. She remembered that I had been in the office, so she stopped me and told me her problem. Her name is Iva Roper and she's a combination nurse-housekeeper for Mrs. Severson, whose son vanished along with George Williams. She is very upset because Harry won't file a report. She told me that Mr. Severson takes care of his mother, who is an invalid, when she is off duty. He cooks his mother's breakfast and takes her in her wheelchair for outings every morning and evening, and spends most of his hours away from work with her."

While Blondie is talking, I walk to the sink as quietly as possible, rinse my dirty dishes, then lean against the counter as she finishes her story. The old feeling in my gut takes over and I know I am one hundred percent correct when I speak. "Blondie, there is no doubt in my mind, and I mean *no doubt*, that we are dealing with a case of double homicide."

# CHAPTER FIVE

MONDAY MORNING, I HIT THE *ARIZONA REPORTER* headquarters a little after eight. Here is where all the action takes place at one of America's great newspapers. I stop at my desk and pick up on my phone messages, then go to the office of our Editor, Ralph 'Specs' Bornheim. As a reporter, Specs never had the big story or the big headline. To be honest, he was just a journeyman reporter. David V. Sacks, who owns and publishes the *Reporter*, saw that his real forte was as an editor, so he got him off the street and behind a desk. I realize that I am a bit of a rebel and that Specs resents rebels. Of course, as long as I keep turning in the headline stories, hitting the national wire with solid syndicated pieces and winning awards, my boy Specs can only look disgusted and grumble.

He's sitting behind his big desk, black horned rim glasses framing his flashing eyes, and he listens with a sour look on his face as I fill him in.

"Look Specs, I'm telling you: this Acme Auto story is going to turn into a red hot case. We're talking about a double homicide."

The face scowls and his lips spit his reply. "My name is not 'Specs' and this is not a homicide case. I've already spoken with Deputy Morse, and as far as George Williams being a missing person, the whole thing's a joke. Get over to the courthouse and get a hold of a story that's really a story."

Specs is not aware of it, but I have just tuned him out. "Of course, Specs—uh, I mean Mr. Bornheim. I'm off to the courthouse."

I opened his door halfway then get in my parting shot.

"I'm going to get a *real* story."

I slam the door behind me. I can picture Specs jumping in his chair.

———

I find what passes for my car downstairs and get the heap in motion. I work my way through traffic out to the Acme Auto Agency.

The daytime temperature is starting to heat up and the cool interior of the agency feels good. As I start through the showroom, a smiling Bill Broaddus comes to meet me.

"Good morning, Mr. McLain. I had a feeling I might be seeing you today."

"Well, Mr. Broaddus, your ESP is certainly in working order. I need your help. Do you have a home address for both Williams and Severson?"

Broaddus looks pleased with himself as he reaches to the inside pocket of his natty white blazer. "I knew you would be back. I have the information you are requesting right here on this card."

He hands me a neatly typewritten card with the data I need to find the homes of both Williams and Severson. I stick the card in my pants pocket, then ask the question that has been floating around on that tape recorder in my mind.

"I was wondering if there's anything at all that you noticed about the young client who took the demo ride? Something you might not have remembered before."

His mental marbles roll around for a couple of seconds. "I'm sure it's not important, but I do remember George and the client got to talking about football while they were waiting for Severson to clear off his desk. This young guy, the client, claimed to have been a hot-shot high school quarterback."

"So, he's a former high school quarterback. There's lots of those around."

"That's true, but this young man said he was a left-handed quarterback and he drove other teams crazy. You have to admit you don't see too many quarterbacks who are left handed."

"By any chance, did he mention that he might be going out for varsity football at Arizona State?"

"Funny you ask. George asked him if he was on the ASU squad and he said no. He claimed to have been burned out on athletics by the end of his high school career and had no desire to compete at the college level."

"Well, Mr. Broaddus, at least we know a little bit about your client, but not enough to get excited."

# CHAPTER SIX

SOMEONE IN THE GEORGE WILLIAMS FAMILY MUST HAVE A love affair with wind chimes. They are everywhere along the rim of the front porch, making tinkling sounds in the hot desert air. On a radio, somewhere inside the house, the song "Autumn Leaves" is playing. The melody mingles with the sound of the chimes.

I punch the doorbell and wait. I punch it again, and wait. One more time, with no success. At last, I bang my fist on the frame of the screen door and yell, "Anybody home?"

A woman, who has traces of beauty, but who has been on the fast track of life, pushes open the screen door. She looks to be about 5'3", maybe 115 pounds with thick blonde hair that hangs to her shoulders, and green eyes. I would guess her age to be around thirty-five. She wears a form fitting dress that accents her figure. A cigarette dangles from her rouged lips and the smoke curls up into the thick hair. This would be an attractive package to any man from sixteen to eighty. However, it's the emerald green eyes that fascinate me. They're knowing. I have the feeling she's seen everything. There is a flicker of suspicion that moves behind them.

"Mrs. Williams? I'm Gene McLain of the *Arizona Reporter*. I wonder if you could tell me where I can find your husband."

She looks me up and down as though I'm a stud horse that she's considering buying. Taking the cigarette from her mouth, she blows the smoke in my direction.

"Yeah, I'm Rosemary Williams, and I have no idea where George might be. If I had to guess, I would say he's gambling and fooling around with some very young ladies in Mexico. George going on a couple of toots a year has been the story of our married life. The lure of booze, gambling, and easy women is something he can't resist."

I have the distinct feeling that Mrs. Williams isn't worried if her husband ever comes back or not, but I push on. "There has been talk of a Missing Persons report being filed on your husband."

She gives a bitter laugh, takes a drag on her cigarette and blows more smoke in my face. "That has to be Billy Broaddus, the owner of Acme Auto. George must be driving one of his fancy new models and he's worried about the merchandise. From personal experience, I can tell you that Billy Broaddus is *only* interested in merchandise."

I try to get matters off a personal track, although I file away what she has told me. "I understand Mr. Broaddus being concerned about his car."

"You got a smart mouth, McLain. I'm not sure you're my kind of man."

I would love to know what the qualifications are for "her kind of man," but I wait for her to continue.

"Why don't you tell Billy not to worry? George is a big, tough guy and can take care of himself. He'll be back when he gets back, and that could be today, tomorrow, or next month."

She puts the cigarette back in her red lips and lets it dangle. She does the up and down look again as if I'm being selected or rejected to be a super stud. In a second, I find that rejection is my fate.

"Do me a favor, McLain. Don't bother me again." She turns and walks into the house. The door is slow closing and I have ample time to admire the roll of her lush hips. Just like in the movies. She gets lost in the darkness of the interior and I'm left standing looking at the closed screen door while the wind chimes flutter and tinkle in a breeze that grows hotter by the minute.

In the back of my head my brain is playing a little warning refrain: remember McLain, she called him "Billy" and indicated he might know more about her "*merchandise*" than one would expect. Husbands have been bumped off for a wide variety of reasons and passion is high on the list. I better do some checking into the private life of one William Broaddus.

# CHAPTER SEVEN

THIS WORN OUT HEAP OF MINE MAKES ME FEEL LIKE I'M IN A sauna. Dick Minton, the mechanic who keeps this pile of metal running, tells me that in a couple of years the Nash/Kelvinator corporation will introduce the automobile industry's first compact and affordable single-unit heating and air conditioning system with controls on the dash. Right now, I don't care where the controls will be as long as I can have cool air to battle the daytime desert heat. How can the ace reporter of the *Arizona Reporter* be nothing but a sweat ball making his rounds to get a story? You can bet I'll be at the head of the line for a new Nash when they hit the market.

I drive up North Central through rows of stately palm trees. On my left, I see the sign for the Winter Garden Manor. I go a half a block up the street, make a U-turn, and park by the beautiful green lawn that fronts this lush mini-resort.

Climbing out of my sauna on wheels, I make my way across the lawn to where a young Mexican gardener is working. I ask if he knows where I can find Mrs. Severson and he points toward a large swimming pool. As I approach the pool, I see an elderly lady with snow white hair seated in a wheelchair under a large metal umbrella. A book is in her lap, but she is not reading. She stares straight ahead, lost in thought.

"Mrs. Severson?"

She jerks out of her reverie and fixes me with lovely hazel eyes.

"I'm Gene McLain from the *Arizona Reporter*. I came to talk with you about your son."

A smile warms her lovely face and she indicates a nearby chair that I pull up beside her.

"Mr. McLain, I can't begin to tell you how happy I am that someone wants to talk about my Harold. My nurse and housekeeper, Mrs. Roper, has tried three times to file a Missing Persons Report, but no one will listen. They say it's because they think that Harold is with a Mr. Williams from the auto agency."

I take her frail hand in mine and make an effort to turn on all of my Irish charm. "Mrs. Severson, I am well aware of the problems you've had. I've heard about Mrs. Roper's visits to the police and the fact that they will not listen to her request. Why don't you tell me about Harold?"

The lady takes a deep breath then launches into her story. "We have only lived here a little over two months. Harold came out first and got a job with the Acme Auto Agency. He gave up a very good job back in Minneapolis to make this move. He was the manager of a large auto dealership. Harold wants me out of the cold Minnesota winters. Here in Arizona, we have sunshine all year long and he's willing to start his career over so I can enjoy what remains of my life to the fullest. Once he gets established, he's going to buy a home. He and Ruth, his childhood sweetheart, are going to be married. She's a lovely girl and they'll be very happy."

"Mrs. Severson, has your son ever talked about George Williams or, by any chance, has he ever brought him home?"

The answer comes fast as a machine gun. "*No.* I have never met Mr. Williams and I am certain that Harold has never mentioned his name. The police told Mrs. Roper that Harold went to Mexico with Mr. Williams, but I know that he would never do that. You see, Mr. McLain, Harold cooks my breakfast and sometimes, depending on his schedule at the agency, my evening meals. He would never go anywhere unless he had made arrangements for someone to be with me."

I release her hand, lean back in my chair, and let the tape recorder of my mind take a couple of whirls. "Mrs. Severson, do you have a photograph of Harold that I could borrow? I promise, I will take good care of it and I will get it back to you as soon as possible."

She reaches into the wicker bag that is attached to the right side of her wheelchair and comes up with a photo in a leather travel frame. The young man in the photo is good looking with a bright smile. He has that clean cut mid-west look about him.

"This is my favorite, Mr. McLain. Please take good care of it and please, please bring my boy home safe and sound."

# CHAPTER EIGHT

THE PARKING LOT BEHIND THE COURTHOUSE IS JAMMED AND I have to jockey around before I can find a parking spot. I come out of the bright sunshine into the dark basement. After getting my eyes back in focus, I walk to the office of Frank Tucker, the High Sheriff of Maricopa County. Blondie has done some special assignments for the sheriff and we get along. Also, he's always good for "inside" information about what's going on in the police department but stonewalls anyone wanting information regarding anything in his jurisdiction.

I make some small talk with Loretta Caruso, his secretary, then enter Frank's office. Sheriff Tucker is leaning back in his desk chair with his custom-made snakeskin boots resting on the desk as he studies an FBI "Most Wanted" report.

When you see Sheriff Tucker, it's hard to believe. He looks like something out of a Hopalong Cassidy or Lone Ranger movie. A white Stetson sits atop his thick silvery hair. He's wearing a white cowboy outfit decorated with silver conches. A big Colt .45 rests on his right hip. You might be inclined to snicker, but when you notice his six foot, three inch frame, how it's all hard and wiry, and the eyes are an exact replica of the eyes of a Diamondback rattlesnake like they died a thousand years ago—that's when any laughter chokes in your throat.

You have heard his reputation. The High Sheriff *always* gets his man and he *always* brings them back dead. It seems they all "resist arrest."

Tucker lowers the poster and smiles with his lips when he sees me, but the rattlesnake eyes never change. "'Bulldog' McLain, as I live and breathe. Hot on the trail of rough and tough George Williams."

"Sheriff, you can't believe …"

"Oh yes, I can believe. I've heard all about the great missing person's case. I just wish this so-called case was under my jurisdiction. I'm telling you, we'd have some real fun with old George and his wild senoritas. By the way, I was just upstairs and our pal Harry Morse was in a lot of deep conversation with the state's legal star, Mr. William O'Neill, our esteemed District Attorney. From what I gather, O'Neill is all lathered up over the problems caused by George and his latest Mexican adventure."

I have what I came for. "Frank, I'd better get hot and follow all the leads, or Specs will be burning up the phone lines wanting me to file a story, and to date, there is no story. I'll catch you later."

I get out of the sheriff's area fast, tell Loretta I'll see her soon, and grab the elevator up to Harry Morse's floor.

# CHAPTER NINE

I CAN TELL THAT MORSE AND THE DA ARE GOING AT IT hammer and tongs from the volume of their voices. The DA, William O'Neill, has just turned forty. He's handsome, talented, ruthless, and hell bent on being Governor of Arizona. He's six feet tall, broad shouldered with sandy hair and a million dollar smile that makes ladies on the jury melt. He always wears well tailored suits and could pass as a fashion model. As I enter the office, I pick up on Morse's statement.

"I'm telling you, Bill, this has gone all the way up to Chief Bleiler and I'm sick and tired of all this to-do about nothing."

O'Neill looks up as I enter and never misses a beat. "Ah, here's our ace snoop. One of the breeds that always wants to make a capital case out of nothing."

I know O'Neill so I let his little jibe slide off and get in my own dig. "Just trying to dream up some murder cases, Counselor. You and I both know that enough of those Murder One convictions can put you in the Governor's mansion."

Morse is angry and has had enough of O'Neill and me sparring. "Look, O'Neill. I've explained to McLain until I'm blue in the face. It's all so very simple. An ordinary fellow, no name, just an ordinary fellow, walks into the Acme Auto

Agency. This fellow, whose name we don't know, says he is interested in buying a new car and wants a demonstration ride. George Williams is the salesman on duty, so George has him step into a snazzy convertible. Harold Severson asks to ride along with them. So, they take a demo ride. Period, end of story."

I have to cut in. "Harry, that's all well and good, but this happened two weeks ago on a Saturday, and this is Wednesday of the third week and the prospective buyer, George Williams, Harold Severson, and the car, have yet to show up anywhere. So, at the very least, this has to be a missing persons story."

O'Neill, always playing lawyer, has to be the devil's advocate. "McLain, do you think we're dealing with a case of mass murder? After all, we're talking about a tough ex-Highway Patrol Officer who often crosses into Mexico to sample the wild life south of the border. This is a pattern that has gone on for years."

O'Neill has the same smug look he always gets when the jury brings in a guilty verdict.

"The weak link in your case, Counselor, is Severson. He has never failed to take care of his mother." I could have bet a million dollars, and won, that O'Neill would go into one of his famous pouts. When he was a little boy he must have picked up his marbles and gone home if he didn't like the game.

"McLain, I really don't want to hear any more about it. You're an award winning reporter, so go out and dig something up worth talking about." He gives me that sarcastic grin of his, then adds, "You know I'll remember you when I'm running this state, so do a good job."

He goes up the hall whistling "Danny Boy." Harry puts on his reading glasses and turns his attention to the stack of papers on his desk.

# CHAPTER TEN

I DO WHAT I ALWAYS DO WHEN THE WHOLE WORLD IS AGAINST me. I go to Blondie. I take the steps rather than the elevator up one floor to where my wife is working. I catch her eye and give her the high-sign that I want to see her . In a minute or two, she finds me and we slip into a deserted courtroom.

My bride, never one to fool with red tape, gets right to the point. "Gene, I can read you like a book. Things are not going well, and don't try to tell me any different."

"As always, you're one hundred percent right. It's not coming together. Not coming together at all. On the way up here, I learned that the cops will issue a Missing Persons Report, but only because Mrs. Severson is putting the pressure on. Someone at Public Affairs reached the decision that they don't want the radio and TV crowd getting the old lady on the air crying and making the department look like a bunch of cold hearts. To top things off, Specs tells me there is no story. O'Neill and the department tells me there is no story. But, I'm telling you that there is a story, a *big story*. Somehow, I have to find the missing pieces to put this puzzle together."

Blondie puts her arms around me and looks at me with

those baby blue eyes that I can't resist. "Honey, if you say it's a big story, I believe you. By the way, O'Neill had a couple of detectives run a check on George Williams and they feel that George, the client, and Severson went to a local bar, had a few belts and then headed south of the border."

I pull out of her arms and start to pace. Her comments have riled me more than a little and it's time to get back on the job.

"I don't think they know anything. What they're doing is blowing smoke. I saw Mrs. Severson and obtained a photo of her son. I'm going over to the paper to pull one George Williams out of the file and have copies made of both pictures. I'll get up early tomorrow and drive down to Nogales and see my pal Frank Hernandez at the Border Patrol. I want to know if either one of them has crossed into Mexico."

Blondie grabs the door handle and starts to leave. "Do what you have to do. You're a veteran reporter who's more like a cop than a cop. You should be able to fit the pieces together and put this story to rest."

With that remark, she's out the door, and I'm alone in the courtroom. By now, she has infused me with a mixture of anger, desire, and a few other emotions that put me into high gear.

The door opens and she pops her head in. "I guess this means we won't be going to the movies tonight, because you have to get up at the crack of dawn."

Hell. I had forgotten all about the promise I'd made to take her to the movies this evening. "Honey, I'll be honest. I forgot about it. What's the name of that new picture you want to see?"

"'Sunset Boulevard' with William Holden and Gloria Swanson. All the girls say it's terrific."

"Some of the guys at the *Reporter* saw it. They told me it's good. Did you know it's about a writer who gets killed? I can tell you this case is killing me. Look, if your mom can baby sit the boys, you go ahead and see the movie. I need to check out some of William's hangouts, so I'll be running late."

# CHAPTER ELEVEN

I GRAB A HAMBURGER AT THE LEGAL EAGLE. MARY O. ASKS where Blondie is and Jo Oakes takes time out from all the male customers who want exclusive service to try and sell me on cherry pie a la mode. Though it's next to impossible to turn Jo down on anything, I do it. If I don't quit hitting the pie and ice cream, I'm going to have to buy new pants.

I leave my car in the lot and walk up to the Trade Winds, which is located by the Adams Hotel on Central Avenue. The Trade Winds is Arizona's answer to Hawaii. The interior of the club could have come directly from Waikiki. The juke box plays only Hawaiian music and Alfred Apaka, "The Voice of The Islands," is singing the song "Beyond The Reef" as I enter through the bamboo and bead curtains. It's early—there are only a few patrons here. Four or five men and women are talking and laughing at the bar while three couples sit at tables lit by hurricane lamps. I find a seat at the far end of the bar.

"Hey Ernie, got a couple of seconds?" I call out to Ernie Lopacka, the muscular bartender.

Ernie is wearing a beautiful blue and yellow Hawaiian print shirt over white slacks. He flashes a big grin and makes his way to my end of the bar as he wipes his hands on a fresh towel. He sticks out his big paw for a hearty handshake.

"Hey, Bulldog. I've always got time for my friend. Can I get you something cool?"

"How about a tall glass of cold pineapple juice? That should hit the spot. If you can take care of that, I'd like a little information."

Ernie fills a tall glass with ice and pours in the juice. Before coming back, he takes care of a couple customers with a Mai Tai and a bottle of beer. He sets the juice in front of me on a napkin bordered with green palm trees.

"What can I do for you?"

"I'm looking for our mutual friend George Williams. Has he been in recently?"

Ernie wipes the bar with his towel.

"George? Gee, I haven't seen him for, um, I guess at least four weeks. He must be doing his thing down in Mexico. Otherwise, he's in here at least a couple of times a week."

I finish my juice and stand. "Thanks, Ernie. Should George show up, will you give me a call at the paper?"

"No problem. I'll let you know if I see him."

I have to step to one side to let a couple enter. As I exit through the bamboo and beads I realize that Alfred Apaka is singing, "I Wish They Didn't Mean Goodbye.",


I walk back to the courthouse and pick up my car. Downtown is quiet, but I know where the action is. This is one of those desert evenings when I wish I had a convertible. What a joy it would be to put the top down and look straight up at the super bright stars, while the desert breezes remind me that I really live in paradise.

# CHAPTER TWELVE

I TAKE IT SLOW DRIVING UP NORTH CENTRAL. I COULD MAKE the Concho Room of the Westward Ho Hotel, but I can't remember ever seeing George there. I pull into the parking lot at Durant's Restaurant and slip in through the kitchen to say hello to my favorite chef, Jim Yancy. Harry Wolf, who makes the greatest Caesar Salads anywhere, pops into the kitchen long enough to say hello and tell me that Jack Durant is up front greeting the customers.

Jack is tall and slender. His hair, which he wears longer than the current fashion, is turning grey on the sides and gives him a distinguished look. I always call him "Smilin' Jack," but that's just a needle. I have never seen Jack smile. One of the cops told me that Jack smiled the night he belted his wife in the chops, but I don't believe it. I do know he had been a top gambler and later a pit boss at the Flamingo in Las Vegas. Jack McElroy, one of the Flamingo owners, brought him to Phoenix. McElroy bought this joint and put Jack's name on it and gave it to him to run. It was an instant success. In fact, Bobby C, along with Marty Martell, a superb Mexican-American guitarist/vocalist, opened the place. From day one, it has been one of the top spots in the city. It's a must for the sports crowd and if you look real close every once in a while you can spot one of the members of the mob, a big-shot from Las Vegas or Hollywood, among the clientele.

Jack is his usual cheerful self when I ask him when he last saw George Williams.

"I saw him four weeks ago Thursday night. I got him involved in a big poker game with some friends of mine from Vegas and they're still holding his IOU for seven thousand dollars."

"Wow, I didn't know George gambled that kind of money."

"McLain, I'm not sure you know anything about George Williams. He not only gambles big, he wins big. You won't find old George on the wrong end of a losing hand very often."

"You sound worried that he left your friends with paper rather than cash."

"I'm not worried at all. George will be good for the money; I have no doubt about that. I'm put out with him because it's evident he's taken off to Mexico on another wild binge. He could have paid the guys before he left rather than when he comes back."

"So, you think George is in Mexico."

"Hell yes. If you knew anything about George Williams you'd know that right this second he's shacked up with a curvy Mexican girl telling lies and making love. I've got to get to work—keep my staff on the ball."

Jack takes off at a brisk pace as he moves into the restaurant. I go out the front door and walk to the back parking lot to pick up my wheels.

I'm getting one hundred percent feedback that George Williams is in Mexico. Could it be that I'm the one in left field and that all these other people are right?

I get back on North Central and drive by Cathy Gardens. I check the rear view mirror to be certain no cops are in sight, then make a fast U-turn, pull in the drive and give the valet my car.

Cathy Gardens was once a large private residence. It is now one of the smartest supper clubs in town. A large one-sheet proclaims that the Fabulous Four Deals, Capital recording stars, are appearing nightly. I met the Deals at KPHO-TV where they provide the musical backup for Bobby C on his TV show. Lloyd Ellis, their fabulous guitar playing leader, is being billed "The Fastest Guitar Alive." The group has a super smooth blend on both instrumentals and vocals.

I can hear them playing and singing one of their original tunes, "Too Late Now." I go up the stairs and look over the crowd.

In a few seconds, I'm joined by club manager Sammy Wong.

"Gene, I'm happy to see you. It's been a while since you were here."

"Sammy, I just don't find time to get around much, but I can tell you I've missed your great food."

"Let me have Kim set up a table for you."

"Don't tempt me. I'm working on a story and I have to keep moving. Sam, has George Williams been around the last couple of weeks?"

"I haven't seen George since the night the Four Deals opened and that was four weeks ago. He was here with a very young and pretty Mexican girl. They were here until closing and drank a lot of champagne. I've not seen him since. If I had to guess, I would say he's in Mexico. You know George."

"Yeah, Sam, I know him. If he comes in, please give me a call at the paper."

"Gene, why don't you pick a date and bring Blondie in for dinner and a show? Everything on the house."

"Sammy, I'll tell Blondie about your kind invitation. We'll get back to you and give you a date and time."

· · ·

I slow down as I pass Joe Hunt's Steak House and, though it is a hotspot in Phoenix nightlife, featuring the jazz guitar of the sensational Howard Roberts, I don't think George Williams is a regular. I turn right onto Camelback Road and I'm greeted by the marquee of the Sundown Club, announcing in blazing lights that the headliner is the fabulous Helen O'Connell with Jack La Delle and Ken Kennedy also appearing. The parking lot shows the place is packed.

The greeter at the front door remembers me, so I walk in without waiting. I hear Miss O'Connell singing "Green Eyes," and the applause that greets the close of that number rocks the house. She announces she will be back in an hour with her second show.

I find Chuck Hurt, the manager, and ask my same questions and get the same answers. "What's wrong with you man? George Williams is in Mexico."

I don't wait to catch Jack La Delle, who plays thirty-two instruments and has a great singing voice, or Ken Kennedy's acts. I've seen both several times before. Plus, they do regular television shots. I get my wheels back from the valet and navigate out to 24th and Camelback to the new "in" spot in Phoenix: the Arizona Manor Hotel, with its Clown's Den Lounge.

# CHAPTER THIRTEEN

THE CLASSY, MULTI-COLORED BILLBOARD PROCLAIMS THAT "Arizona's Brightest Television Star, the one and only Bobby C, is appearing nightly. Plus, for three evenings only, a true musical legend will appear, Rudy Vallee. I push my way into the packed house. Though I don't have him in my vision, I can hear Rudy going into the last eight bars of "As Time Goes By," the unforgettable song from the classic movie "Casablanca." Applause and cheers drown out everything else at the close of the song. Bobby C does a sparkling arpeggio on the keyboard and Rudy launches into a few bars of his theme song, "My Time Is Your Time," as I break through the crowd..

At last, I work my way to the end of the room where Bobby, backed by the smooth guitar of Marty Martell, is winding up a swinging chorus of "Rose Room." I slide onto the treble side of the piano bench just as Bobby announces there will be more music in fifteen minutes. He snaps off his microphone and pushes it away. Though he has announced a break, he still doodles on the keys as we talk. I notice that he's sweating, but he seems very happy with the way things are going.

"How's the king of the keyboard?"

"To be honest, between my six day a week television show and this gig, I'm a little tired."

A sweet young thing passes by the Steinway grand and, with a smile, she murmurs, "Bobby, you're just wonderful."

I can see this is really tough work, so I have to get a little dig in just to keep Bobby on his toes. "Outside of trying to become the richest entertainer in Arizona, why don't you give up the club life and stick to TV?"

What the boys down at the police station call a "de-icer" interrupts our chat. Her cocktail dress is cut almost lower than the law allows. Her breasts are large and tan and above those charms is a pixie face with short black hair and lilac eyes. "I have to leave for a while, but I'll be back before closing."

Bobby, who is never slow on the up-take, snaps back, "Okay, Helen. I'll be looking for you." He says this while giving her a big, slow wink. It makes me wish I had taken piano lessons. This looks like a job for any red-blooded American gentleman. Bobby follows her walk until she is lost in the crowd, then turns back to me as if our conversation has been a steady flow. "In answer to your question, I'm hooked on the clientele."

"Yeah, I can see the clientele is first rate."

"No, no, not the girls. They're everywhere. I'm talking about the celebrity guests. This is *the* in place in this city. One of these days, I'm going to write a book and a great deal of the material will come from what I have seen and heard right in this room. For example, did you know that Walter Winchell and Groucho Marx are here most weekends? Last week, Jack Kogen, the boss, had me go down to one of the bungalows to provide background music during a *very* private dinner for none other than Howard Hughes and his current lady friend. In fact, the lady friend, Janis Page, is a young movie star and has her picture plastered on just about every screen magazine in the world as 'the girl who has never been kissed.' I can tell you, my friend, there was plenty of kissing and romance with Mr. Hughes."

I can't help but laugh. Bobby, who is dead serious, sounds like a male version of Hedda Hopper or Louella Parsons. "Bobby you're really living in the fast lane. Since you have the pulse of this place, was the ladies favorite, George Williams, in last Saturday evening with this man?" I have a wallet size duplicate of the photo that Mrs. Severson loaned me, and I hand this to the wizard of the eighty-eight keys. He stops doodling as he takes a good hard look at the photo. Shaking his head, he hands the picture back and starts softly fingering the keyboard.

"I never saw that guy in my life, but I did see George last Friday."

"Think hard, Bobby. Are you sure it was Friday and not Saturday?"

"No, it was Friday. The reason I can remember is because I had a group of models on my TV show and one of them was really dynamite. I convinced her to have dinner with me after the show was finished. Later, I brought her out here so she could see me work."

He lifted his right hand off the keys to point to a table for two that was just to the right of the big Steinway grand.

"She was sitting right there and at the next table was another real beauty. Big George came in and tried to pick up this hot number, but she was waiting for a guy who was staying here at the hotel. She was trying to ease George down gently when the guy shows up and he and George get into a beef. This guy is as big as George, so it would have been an interesting match, but you know the Chicago crowd keeps things under tight control, and the net result was that they asked George to leave."

"How about that? 'Big George' being asked to leave. I can't imagine that happens too often."

"I was as surprised as you are. George drops a lot of

money in this joint, but the guy he was fooling with is somebody very big from Chicago. In fact, rumor has it that he's going to invest a bundle of dough in this town. I know he asked a lot of questions about the operation of the Greyhound track, and I have the feeling he knows more than normal about all kinds of gambling."

I filed away everything Bobby has said about George and make the decision to skip the Camelback Inn and the Biltmore, two beautiful spots but not the kind of places that George Williams would hang out. I'm going to run back downtown to check if anybody at The Flame has seen my wandering boy. The Hitching Post on Camelback Road and Charley Briley's Pink Pony in Scottsdale will hold until another night. I stand up and look down at "Mr. Smiles."

"Thanks Bobby, I enjoyed our chat, to say nothing of the lovely young ladies who seem to be all hung-up on your keyboard and vocal magic."

Bobby gives me that television grin that the women love. "Just the tricks of the trade, Gene. It's all part of the game."

"You keep the game going, Bobby, but if you happen to see George Williams, please give me a call at the paper. Something has come up and it's important that I find out where he is."

As I move away from the piano, a stunning suntanned blond in a white dress takes my seat on the piano bench. "Bobby, please play the new song you wrote. I just die every time I hear it."

Bobby turns on his big smile, pulls the mike to him and snaps it on. He nods to Marty Martell to give him an intro on the guitar. By the time I fight my way to the exit, he has finished the first chorus of his new tune, "Yellow Roses."

Poor guy. I can tell it's going to be a long, long night.

# CHAPTER FOURTEEN

THE FLAME, AN UPSCALE SPOT IN THE HEART OF DOWNTOWN, IS owned by a classy guy named Lyle Orick who comes from Minnesota. This plush club features a jungle bar that includes live monkeys and exotic birds. They have excellent food and the best dance band in the southwest, Al Overend, and his Orchestra. They're busy with a group vocal of the current hit, "If I Knew You Were Comin' I'd've Baked A Cake."

I say hello to off-duty detective Gordon Selby, who is having dinner with a very pretty dark blonde. Gordon is a real fashion plate on duty or off. He could pass as a twin of movie star Tyrone Power. Punks make the mistake when they think Selby is soft. Too late they discover he's the messenger of death with a gun in his hand.

The dance floor is crowded, and I work my way around it to catch up with Lyle at the kitchen entrance. I ask my questions and get the same old answers.

"I would suspect that George is in Mexico. You know, Gene, he loves that south of the border life."

Before I depart, I check with the bartenders and a couple of waitresses. I get the standard "He's in Mexico" answer.

Enough is enough. Time to go home. My wheels are two

blocks down the street. Passing an alley entrance, I smell a strong odor of vomit, body heat, sweat and rotten garbage. Out of the dark, I hear a familiar raspy voice call my name in a kind of stage whisper, "Hey Bulldog, it's me. I've got something for you."

The voice belongs to Jack 'The Blink' Cutter, a professional snitch who, for a few bucks, has given the cops and yours truly some very accurate tips. The street guys call him "Blink," because the lid of his right eye hangs half shut thanks to the work of a straight razor from a fight down at the big house. This scar runs down into his lip, giving him a look that you find in horror movies. He's sniffling like he has a cold and his face has a week's worth of beard. His ragged clothes and the odor that clings to them smells like a dumpster filled with spoiling meat and fruit.

"I got something for you, Gene, that's maybe worth a couple of bucks."

I look over this filthy piece of humanity whose life is spent moving from flop house to flop house. The one thing he does know is the street, and he's been around long enough to know usable information from trash.

"Okay, Blink. What have you got?"

"A source told me you were interested in knowing about Billy Broaddus and George Williams' wife, Rosemary."

"That's true, if there is anything to know."

He wipes his rheumy eyes, then gets his saw-edged voice into gear. "They had a hot, and I mean a *red hot* affair going for three or four months. The word on the street was that when 'Big George' caught them, somebody was going to get killed. I guess with a sizzling broad like that, Billy felt it was worth the chance, but it's all over. You can check the register at the Night Owl Motel in Chandler. Five weeks ago, a Mr. and Mrs. William Broaddus checked into room six. They had a knock-down, drag-out fight and the way I get it, the fight was over the fact that Rosemary Williams has been making trips up to Las Vegas to share her charms with a mob enforcer named Johnny Saita during the same period she's been romancing Billy. They used to hit motels in Apache Junction, Wickenburg, Litchfield, and other spots just out of town."

I find a fin in my wallet and press it into Blink's grimy hand. He stuffs it into a pocket of his stained and soiled pants.

"Thanks Bulldog, I'll be seeing you." He starts to turn back into the alley when a hot wire goes off in my head.

"Blink, just a second. You may not have any knowledge of this, but do you think that it might be possible that Mrs. Williams would have George killed for his insurance?"

A gurgle that passes for laughter comes from behind his badly decayed teeth. "She would have to be one dumb broad. Everyone knows what George Williams thinks about insurance in general, and people who sell insurance. Hell, Gene, George wouldn't buy a dime's worth of insurance if he knew he was going to die in two minutes."

Amazing what hard cold facts you can learn on the mean streets. I thank 'Blink' and he melts back into the dark alley and is lost from sight. The smell of vomit, rotten meat, and spoiled fruit remain, and I hurry toward my car to lose the odors.

I get behind the wheel and think before taking off. I realize that I can throw out the love triangle of murder for insurance and get back to square one. The missing person's case.

# CHAPTER FIFTEEN

I SET MY MENTAL CLOCK TO BEAT THE ALARM, AND AS I COCK one eye open I can see that the hands say 4:00 AM. I slide out of bed as quietly as possible, so as not to wake Blondie, grab my razor and shaving cream out of our bathroom, then go to the kids bathroom to shower and shave. The way they sleep, you could fire off a bomb and they would never hear it.

I manage to get back to our room and get dressed. I'm very quiet going down the stairs. In the kitchen, I find the coffee, and get our percolator started so that Blondie will wake up to the smell of good dark coffee brewing. I let myself out the side door, get the engine started, and slowly roll my car out into the street. Everything is silent. The first light of dawn is just breaking over the mountains as I head south.

I know that the politicians have been discussing the advantages of building some sort of super highway that will link Phoenix to Tucson and Nogales, and that could happen in a few years, but even if they build it, I'll still use the current road. I love this two lane highway. Maybe it's the kid in me that thrills to the many dips in the road that often has a sprinkle of desert sand covering the blacktop.

Over the years, I have figured out the correct speed to hit the dips without having an accident. You're going straight across the desert, then without warning you go into a steep dip. In most cases the rise on the other side of the dip is quite sharp. If your front bumper hits the dip on the way up, the chances of having your car overturn, suffering major injuries or death, is quite possible. In fact, that's what killed the famous cowboy movie actor, Tom Mix. Tom was flying over this highway when he went into a sudden dip. The front of his big touring car hit the highway on the way up and that ended the career of a film legend. I always stop by the stone memorial that has been placed beside the highway where Mix died. There, you can look forever over the endless desert to the faraway mountains. I wonder what Tom's last thoughts might have been. Or did it happen so fast that there were no thoughts?

Arizona has a lot of crosses by the side of the highways where people have died in accidents. For the most part, the crosses are neglected and some have rotted away or disappeared, but this two lane road could tell a million tales of old Arizona.

I stop for gas at Oracle Junction, then hit the road again. Within a few miles, I see the start of the Santa Catalina Mountain range, which is part of the Coronado National Forest. The mountains rise more than 9000 feet above the desert floor and this is the site of famous Mt. Lemon. From the top, the ski runs have a vertical drop of 870 feet. Mt. Lemon Lodge is a delightful place in the summer when those who are so inclined can enjoy horseback riding and hiking in cool weather while the valley below is sweltering.

The rumbling in my stomach reminds me that I haven't had breakfast. Before hitting Tucson, I pull off at a small cafe that looks neat and clean, and have a wonderful Arizona breakfast of Huevos Rancheros and good Mexican coffee.

Tucson, which is the second-largest city in Arizona, is a lot higher in elevation than Phoenix. The area rises from the floor of the Sonoran Desert with five mountain ranges. They reflect color tones different from those found anywhere else. This city has managed to retain a magical mix of historical romance and modernism. Southwest of the city, I pass the world famous mission, San Xavier del Bac (the White Dove of the Desert), located on the San Xavier Indian Reservation. It continues the legacy of the Spanish missionary, Father Kino. A little farther, on my right, is the Tubac Presidio State Historic Park. That's the location of the Presidio Museum where the Spanish established a garrison after the massacre of settlers in 1751. Tubac became the first European settlement in what is now Arizona.

A few miles north of Nogales is the Tumacacori National Monument. There are partially restored ruins of a mission church built by the Franciscans in 1800, which was then abandoned due to Indian uprisings. I'm now just eleven miles from the border, and on my right is Rio Rico. Rumor has it that a big chain is going to build a hotel there on the mesa.

I enter the American side of Nogales. The twin cities of Nogales-Arizona and Sonora, Mexico feature modern day buildings, but still keep the exotic spell of Old Mexico complete with shopping, night life, Mexican food, parades, fiestas, and bullfights. I melt into the line of traffic headed for the border checkpoint. It's stop and go, at a snail's pace, until at last the Border Patrol station comes into view. I pull out of the traffic and cut into a space reserved for patrol cars.

I find my old friend, Captain Frank Hernandez, a Mexican-American who was born in the tiny town of Globe, Arizona. He does a fantastic job of handling all the problems that are daily occurrences with people and materials going from one country to another. Frank is a good looking, well-built gentleman who just turned thirty-eight. He has a big bear hug for me and it takes a second to get my breath back.

I give him copies of the photos of George Williams and Harold Severson and he hands them to one of his staff to pass around to the people currently on duty, then turns his attention to me.

"After your call yesterday, I asked everyone I work with and left a memo for the other two shifts to let me know if George Williams has crossed into Mexico or the US in the last two or three weeks. We have an advantage regarding Williams because almost everyone who works here remembers George from his days on the Highway Patrol. Also, when he comes through, which can be every week during bullfighting season, he always shoots the breeze with some of the guys and tries his moves on some of my gals."

"As I told you, Frank, something inside me tells me that neither George nor this Severson fellow ever went to Mexico. However, this is the only answer I get from all the investigation I've done. It's the same answer from the police, his boss, his wife, everyone. 'Don't get excited—George is in Mexico.'"

Frank sits on the edge of his desk. "I'm going to send copies of both photos to all the ports of entry both in Arizona and California, just to have all the bases covered. I doubt that they would enter Mexico anywhere except here. It's the most direct route, so why go out of their way?"

"I don't think they ever went to Mexico, but by covering all the ports of entries in both states, the cops can't say the coverage wasn't complete."

"Gene, can you stick around and have a late lunch? I'm running a little shorthanded today and won't be able to break until around three o'clock."

"I'd love to, but I had better head for Phoenix. It's just my luck that Williams might turn up or something important breaks, and since it's my story, I want to be in on the wrap-up."

"Adios, Bulldog. Give your beautiful wife a hug and a kiss for me. I'll keep on top of the situation at this end of the line."

# CHAPTER SIXTEEN

HEADING BACK TO THE VALLEY OF THE SUN, I ONCE AGAIN take the two lane road heading north. I don't get that much of a chance to drive the dips anymore, so I have to take my shot when opportunity knocks. My internal message tape plays a word of warning. "If you're heading down this way, or for that matter any road across the desert, and you drive down in dips or washes, be certain you look both ways. You'll get the surprise of your life if you see a wall of water coming straight at you out of a bone dry desert."

There's no warning of a flash flood and only quick action on your part can save your life. Just a couple of years ago, some friends of mine were hit by one of the flash floods and they have never found the car, the wife, and the two daughters. The husband survived by being thrown from the car, but you can be certain it changed his life forever.

So, with my head turning right and left as I go down and up the dips, I head for home.

# CHAPTER SEVENTEEN

For no explainable reason, I make a stop at the Arizona State Prison located on the banks of the Gila River. It's a tough prison, maybe the toughest in the USA.

I'm ushered into a large office. Warden Franks comes around his desk to meet me. Six foot one, he's a fit and trim fifty-five years old with the build of a middle linebacker. His close cropped hair is silver and his eyes have a steely glint.

"This visit is unexpected. I haven't seen you since the Gonzales brothers were executed. What brings you down to this heavenly spot on the beautiful Gila River?"

I have to laugh, since the "beautiful Gila River" only has water in it during flood time. "I'm on my way back to Phoenix. I spent the morning with Frank Hernandez down at the Border Patrol, trying to find out if a couple of missing men had entered old Mexico."

The Warden leans back in his high backed leather chair, looks at the ceiling, then fixes me with that steely gaze.

"Now this wouldn't have anything to do with George Williams and a fellow named Severson, would it?"

You can't put anything over on the Warden. "To tell the truth, it does, but how did you know?"

"New arrivals come down every few days from Maricopa County. While they're guests at your jail, they talk to cops and to other felons, and they may know more about the Phoenix Police Department than the Department knows about itself. I heard the story from one of my trustees three weeks ago. Since I know George Williams, it piqued my interest."

"Do any of your guests have theories as to what happened to the men in question?"

"According to the cons, they feel that a person or persons unknown may have committed the perfect crime. They debunk any stories that the two men are in Mexico. As you well know, there's lots of holes out in the desert, and the guys you're looking for may be filling one or two of them."

What the Warden says makes sense. I thank him for his views and ask him to call me if he hears anything concrete.

# CHAPTER EIGHTEEN

IT'S COCKTAIL HOUR BY THE TIME I PULL INTO SCOTTSDALE, A Phoenix suburb that likes to pretend it's not a part of greater Phoenix, but a separate oasis for the famous and wealthy who own beautiful homes in the area. A couple of years ago someone wrote a book titled "Gold Cadillac Town" in which the author proclaimed this lovely place as the wife swapping capital of America.

I park down the street from Don Fredrick's gas station. It's built in what is reputed to be a frontier motif, and walk up the wooden sidewalk to Charley Briley's famous Pink Pony, Scottsdale's favorite watering hole.

Some people want to win Academy Awards, or Nobel Prizes, or to be on the covers of world renowned magazines, but if you live in Scottsdale, your social status has reached its peak only if your caricature hangs framed on the walls in the Pink Pony.

The place is going full blast. As I look for a seat, I spot a lot of folks whose likenesses adorn the walls. I edge my way onto a stool between a curvy redhead who has seen the plastic surgeon on at least a couple of occasions, and a pale visitor who is wearing a cowboy hat pretending to be the reincarnation of Wyatt Earp. I'd like to tell him that if he wants to talk about the frontier Marshall, who was really a fast gun and cleaned up the outlaws in Arizona, he would be talking about John Slaughter. However, I pass on the chance to set history straight.

While waiting for the bartender to bring libation for my dry and thirsty throat, I let my eyes wander over the sketches behind the bar. Down on the left hand side, with a smile a yard wide, is a drawing of George Williams. The harried bartender arrives and I order a tall gin and tonic. When it comes, I lift my glass in a silent salute to George and wonder if he's smiling wherever he is now. I order another, and when it arrives, I drink slowly and one by one crush the ice cubes in my teeth.

Looking over the room, it reads like a "Who's Who". I catch sight of Charley Briley, the owner himself, coming through the door. He has a lot of hands to shake and backs to slap while passing out good wishes before he turns toward the bar. I leave what's left of my drink and work my way through the layers of laughing and drinking humanity, so that I can intercept him.

"Good God, the one and only Bulldog McLain. I haven't seen you in ages. There must be a murder in our little town. I just hope none of my patrons have been deep sixed."

Charley is a good guy and his business is clean and solid. He passed me some vital information on a murder case a couple of years back and I have always been grateful.

"I hope I'm not working on a murder case. However, I'm trying to find the whereabouts of George Williams, former hero of the Highway Patrol."

"I haven't seen George in over a month. That's not unusual. I'm sure you know more about his trips to Mexico than I do. When he's in town, he hits here at cocktail time or early evening at least three days a week. In fact, there are several local ladies who are most anxious for George to return.

I don't know what he has, but you've got to admit he has something."

"Charley, everyone from the Governor to the newsboy on the street tells me that George is in Mexico. I just wish he'd show up and prove that all of them are right."

Charley offers to buy me a drink, but I've had my limit. I say Adios and get in my heap and head for home sweet home. First, I need to stop at the Hitching Post which is located on a canal bank just about halfway down Camelback Road toward Central Avenue.

Tony, the owner, is a fine Italian gentleman who has turned this rustic place into a favorite for the locals. He features a piano bar and Tony himself loves to sing "Oh Marie" and "O Sole Mio" for the guests. I understand that George Williams, who I am told has a pretty good baritone voice, likes to take over the mike and give the crowd his imitation of Frank Sinatra.

Tony is getting ready for the evening crowd but sits down with me. He offers me a glass of wine and a plate of pasta, but I tell him Blondie will have something good waiting for me. I just want a few seconds of his time. I want information regarding our mutual friend George Williams, and also to see if he could identify Harold Severson from the photo I carry with me.

No, he has never seen Severson, and he has not seen George for at least six weeks. Of course he is not alarmed, because everyone knows that Mr. Williams has to be in Mexico. Okay, McLain, time to hang it up for this long day.

# CHAPTER NINETEEN

THE COPS HAVE A RULE OF THUMB THAT HAS PROVED TO BE quite accurate. If a homicide isn't solved, or if you fail to generate a hot lead within forty-eight hours, the odds are that the case will never be solved. As the weeks have turned into months I'm very much aware that the case of the missing salesmen has faded from the memories of the public.

This morning's staff meeting at the *Reporter* with Specs playing cheerleader tells us there is a small dip in the circulation. This, of course, is the fault of less than brilliant reporting. He glares at me as he remarks that some of the reporters are spending time on nowhere stories instead of digging for first class material. The Society Editor looks as though she may cry, while it is all I can do to keep from laughing at this entire scene. After the rah-rah, I check all my messages and make the needed calls.

I wish I knew what I was looking for. I know I'm restless, I'm frustrated, and I feel like my head is getting sore beating it against a wall with this missing persons case. I wander through various offices at the courthouse looking for—hell—I don't know what I'm looking for. I glide into Marge Kratzer's domain. Marge is a tiny bundle of energy. Pretty, with a cute figure and warm smile. She's putting a stack of reports in wire baskets to go to various departments.

"Ah ha, the people's choice, our favorite newspaper reporter, the one and only Gene McLain."

"Hi, Marge. Is there anything that might attract the attention of a tired reporter?"

"Funny thing: I was considering calling you at the paper and you wander in. Our ESP must be working."

Marge is a very smart girl and she must have something good. "What have your pretty eyes discovered?"

She digs through a pile of paper on her desk and comes up with a Phoenix Police Department report sheet. "I want you to look at this. This is the report of an abandoned 1940 Ford. It was left on a canal bank about a hundred yards from Van Buren Street. I gather it has been there for quite some time. I know you're looking for a 1950 Ford convertible and this is certainly not it. This car is ten years old. What's really strange is that the license plates and registration are missing, but the key was still in the ignition and the gas tank was two thirds full."

She hands me the report and I scan the details.

"This is really strange."

"Buddy Carroll was the reporting officer. Do you want me to have him call you?"

I hand the report back. "No need to have Buddy call. By any chance, do you happen to know which impound lot has the car now?"

"The tow truck took it to West Side Salvage."

I lean over the desk and give Marge a kiss on the cheek, making her blush. "You're a sweetheart, Marge. Thanks for the information. I'm on my way."

West Side Salvage is a junk man's dream. The lot is jammed with cars both old, new and in between. Joe Terzian, who owns the yard, takes me to where they have dumped the 1940 Ford that has been abandoned. "This is the baby, Gene.

Nothing unusual about it except the plates and the registration are missing. It's in pretty good shape for a ten year-old car. Not too many miles, and the engine looks almost like new."

"Joe, this could be important on a case I'm working on. Do you have any objections if I go through this car with a fine tooth comb?" Joe gives me a friendly grin. "Gene, if you want to tear it apart, be my guest. The car won't go back on the market. It's going to be sold for parts, so see what you can find."

Joe wanders out through the yard and I get to work. Believe me, if ever a car got torn apart from stem to stern, it's this poor old Ford. The afternoon is a scorcher and by five I am hot, dirty and about ready to go out of my mind with frustration.

Joe steps up behind me. When he speaks, he gives me a start. "How's it going, Gene? Have you found anything that gives you a hot lead?"

I rub at the dirt and grime covering my face. "Not a thing. This car is clean as a whistle. I'll write down the motor number. Maybe this will throw some light on the subject. By the way, thanks for the use of your tools and space."

"Anytime, Gene. Just sorry you couldn't find something concrete. Get a good cold shower and you'll feel better."

I take a shower, first hot, then cold. Afterwards, I feel like a new man. Blondie calls to let me know she has to work late. We make a date to meet for dinner at The Flame in an hour. I decide to make good use of the time by having a talk with Morse.

## CHAPTER TWENTY

THE SUN IS SETTING AS I ARRIVE AT HARRY'S OFFICE. HE spots me before I get through the open door. "McLain, you better start wearing a hat. You've been in the sun too long and your brain is getting baked."

If he thought my brain was baked before, he's certain he's right after I tell him about the 1940 Ford I spent the better part of the day dismantling. "Harry, I'm telling you that this car is somehow tied to the car used on the demo ride at the Acme Auto Agency."

Harry is reaching the end of his severely strained patience. "Just what or who tells you that these cars have anything to do with each other?"

"Harry, it's my gut. My intuition. It tells me these two are tied together and my instinct has never been wrong."

He looks at me with the same distaste he would should Adolph Hitler return to the world of the living. "Get out of here. Forget this whole situation and go take a look at the new stuff coming in. Can't you get it through your head that you're beating a dead horse?" He pulls a stack of papers toward him, reaches in a side drawer, and brings out his reading glasses. I start out the door, but he stops me.

"By the way, Bulldog, your editor has been trying to reach you. When you talk to him, please tell him that I'm not running an answering service for his newspaper."

# CHAPTER TWENTY-ONE

TELL ME, WHERE DID THE PAST WEEK GO? HERE IT IS Saturday morning at the McLain household and our sons Larry and Jerry are seated at the kitchen table with their Dad, while Blondie works her culinary magic making waffles, frying bacon and eggs while keeping our plates full of good hot food. I offer to help, but have been instructed to sit down and enjoy. The kids and I have laid waste to everything in sight. Little Jerry is the first to finish and he launches the attack with the question I've been dreading.

"Dad, you promised that you'd take us to the park today, right?"

Larry picks up the ball as quick as a wink. "Yeah, Dad. This is Saturday, remember? You said you wouldn't have to work and that you'd spend the day with us. Right, Mom?"

Blondie comes over to the table and puts her hands on my shoulders. "Boys, please! Daddy's had something very important come up that he has to take care of. You go out and play and then I'll take you to the park. Daddy will join us later."

Wonder of wonders, the boys accept this and jump up from the table and make a rush for the back door. I take my wife's hand and pull her down on my lap.

"You saved me again. I get so tired of being the bad guy, but I just have to get over to the DMV before they close at noon to see Dick Smith and get him to research the sale of a 1940 Ford, in case it was sold in Arizona. There's no logical reason that someone would buy a car, then leave it with a tank full of gas and the key in the ignition."

"You know, Gene, it's quite possible that this car was bought someplace else and then the owner, for whatever reason, abandoned it here."

"I grant you, that's possible, but I have to find out and quickly. Specs is really putting the pressure on me to drop this case, so I've got to try and find out all I can while I can."

Blondie pours a cup of coffee and takes a sip. "Do you remember what registration forms looked like in 1940? Were they different or do they still use the same form?"

I pick up my dishes and take them to the sink to rinse. "No, why do you ask?"

"I wonder if there is any way you could pass a ten year-old registration form off as a new one."

"I have no idea, sweetheart, but when I talk with Dick, I'll ask him to dig up a couple of old forms and we'll take a look."

Blondie takes the dishes from me and gives me a kiss. "Okay Bulldog, go get 'em, but don't forget you have two sons who will be waiting for you at the park. You know they really want and value time with you."

# CHAPTER TWENTY-TWO

THE LIGHTS ARE ON IN OUR KITCHEN AND THE RADIO IS TUNED to KOOL and "The Sheldon Gibbs Ranch Show." Marty Robbins is singing "Raindrops On My Window, Teardrops In My Heart," a song that Bobby C wrote. There's a knock at the back door. Blondie opens it to reveal Dick Smith, age sixty, tall and slender with excellent features, a great head of white hair and a winning smile.

"Good evening, Ms. McLain. I'm Dick Smith from the DMV. I told Gene I would drop by with the information he requested."

"Come in and sit down, Mr. Smith. Let me get you a cup of coffee and a slice of wonderful Mexican wedding cake with pure vanilla icing. My mother brought it over this afternoon and I've already sampled a slice."

Dick takes a seat at the table, but puts his hands up in protest. "I'm certain the cake is delicious, but please, nothing for me. It's our anniversary and I promised my wife I'd take her for a steak dinner at Durant's. I don't want anything to spoil that."

"Congratulations on your anniversary. Gene will be down in a second. He just finished showering. He and the boys had quite a day at the park. The boys—grandma took them to her house for dinner. I bet they're sound asleep by now."

I come through the door just in time to hear the end of Blondie's statement. "I can tell you they sure wore their Dad out. Now I know why you have children when you're young."

"I know how you feel, Gene. I sure miss having my boys at home, but I have an awful lot of fun when the grandchildren come to visit."

Dick hands me the brown envelope that he has in front of him. "Everything is there that you asked for. By the way, I got lucky and found some old forms, and brought them along. You'll see that the DMV hasn't changed anything." Dick pushes his chair back and stands. "I hate to run, but the missus is waiting for me." He takes a quick look at his watch. "We have a reservation and I don't want to be late."

Blondie walks him to the back door. "You had better not be late for your anniversary. McLain told me that he's taking me out tonight for a romantic dinner, so all of us have important plans. Come back sometime and bring your missus with you."

"Thanks, Mrs. McLain. I know she would like to meet you."

I've been so busy reading the materials that I haven't thanked Dick for his work. "Thanks, Dick. I really appreciate all your efforts."

Blondie closes and locks the door. "I'll run upstairs and get my purse."

This is one of the times when I know I'm married to an angel. I use that fact to take a terrible advantage. "Honey, I've got to go down to headquarters. This car was sold by Desert Star Motors on east Van Buren. I've got to get Harry to go with me on this one." While I'm talking, I take the sales report out and throw the envelope on the table. When I look up, I see my bride looking beautiful with teardrops in her big blue eyes.

"Just a minute, Gene. We have a date this evening. I saved

up to buy this dress for just such an occasion. Mom has the kids and we're going out to dinner. We have the whole evening together, just the two of us."

I admit it. At times like these, I feel like King Rat, but of course I have a typical Irish quip fresh at hand. "Look, sweetheart, just dry your eyes. You're so beautiful in your new dress. I'm so proud of you and lucky to be your husband. I'll be home in nothing flat. Just stay in those beautiful clothes and I'll be right back, then we'll go out on the town."

# CHAPTER TWENTY-THREE

By the time I get to headquarters, Morse is closing his office. He's reaching for the switch to the overhead lights when I rush through the door.

"Hey, McLain, don't you ever go home? It's Saturday night and ..." I'm waving the DMV report in my hand. I cut him off in mid-sentence.

"What about this? What about this report?"

"What report? Don't tell me someone has blown up Goldwater's Department Store."

"Come on Harry, we don't have time for this kind of stuff. Look, a while back, a car was abandoned on a canal bank, the same make of car that George Williams, Harold Severson, and the unknown client disappeared in, and the license plates and the registration are missing. The automobile was sold by Desert Star Used Cars."

To say Harry is irritated is putting it mildly. "Hold it, McLain. I know all about this ten year old car. One of my guys ran it down and I also talked to officer Carroll, who found it. This has *nothing* to do with Williams, Severson, or their client."

Harry flicks off the overhead light and moves toward the

door, but I block his way. "Harry, you're a cop. Don't you get the picture? The unknown client bought this ten year-old car because he wanted the registration and the plates. I don't know how, but there has to be some way he can make the old registration look like new. The license plates are clean, so if he should be stopped he has proof positive that the Ford is his. When he left the keys in the car with a tank half-full of gas, that tells us he just wanted the registration and the license plates. There is no other answer."

Harry gives me the full bore of his most sarcastic voice. "Very good, Gene, very good. Maybe you should be over at NBC in Hollywood writing for Jack Webb. You know, Sergeant Joe Friday on the show 'Dragnet'." Harry then hums the starting notes of the "Dragnet" theme that everyone in America knows by heart. His face flushes with anger and his voice goes up a notch or two. "George Williams is still a mean six-foot-four, and I'm telling you, *there is no connection!*"

I still block the exit to his office.

"Will you come down to Desert Star Used Cars with me?"

"No!""Do you have any objections if I go down?"

"Yes!"

"Well, you can't stop me. I can go anyway."

Harry gives me a shove and exits out the door.

"No, it's a free country, but you won't be seeing anyone there tonight. Just take a look at the clock on the wall. The lot's closed."

# CHAPTER TWENTY-FOUR

THE ONLY LIGHTS ON IN OUR HOUSE ARE IN THE KITCHEN AND a soft wattage in the living room. Opening the kitchen door, I find Blondie in her old robe with a cup of coffee at the kitchen table. She fixes me with those beautiful blue eyes. "Ah, the famous Bulldog Gene McLain. The great lover who promised his wife that he would take her out for dinner and a little romance. Let me tell you something, you don't look like a lover to me."

I knew our planned evening was important to Blondie, but now I know *just* how important it had been. "Honey, there's no words to tell you how sorry I am that I ruined our evening. I know we don't get a whole lot of time without the kids, but I had to see Harry to see if he would help me."

"Don't tell me, the answer was no."

I took my time getting a cup of coffee to hide my embarrassment and anger at the runaround Harry had given me, but I had to confirm what Blondie had told me.

"You're right, as always. The answer was no. He says that the plates and registration being gone mean nothing. He swears there's no connection."

I take my coffee over to the table and sit down opposite my

lovely wife who still puts up with my foolishness after all these years. I notice a little smile playing around her lips, but this is not a time to be smiling.

"How much do you love me?"

"What's wrong with you? You're my little girl and I love you more than anything in the whole world. Even though I break dates, and your heart in the process, I do love you and you know that."

"Well, you better love your wife. I had planned a wonderful evening. A good dinner, a few dances and who knows, maybe a little romance as frosting on the cake. Look at you. You're tired and worn and uncertain where this crazy story is taking you. Let me see a smile on that Irish kisser."

I gulp my coffee and get up to get another cup. "Let's face it, there's nothing to smile about."

"That's where you're wrong. While you were doing your little song and dance for the Phoenix Police Department, your wife was reviving her skills as an artist."

I sit back down at the table asking, "What skills as an artist?"

"How quickly you forget all those hundreds of drawings I used to do, before life in the fast lane with you left me with no time for mundane things. Well, tonight, while you were downtown, once I realized that our plans for the evening were cancelled, I got out my drawing pen and ink and did a little art work on something that just might help my struggling husband."

Blondie held up a DMV registration card. "Look, this is the 1950 registration card for my car."

"So, what's the big deal? The car's not paid for by any means."

"I know that. But look at this." She holds up another registration card and I begin to wonder if Blondie is slipping her cogs, because I've blown the evening and her chance to wear her new dress.

"So, whose registration is that?"

"McLain, that's for you to find out. The important thing is that you're looking at a 1940 registration that has been doctored to become a 1950 registration." I took the paper from her and somewhere the light was starting to go on that my bride is way ahead of my efforts in solving the missing person's caper.

"I can't believe it. I can't tell the difference. How about that? You've given me the key that's going to bust this case wide open."

My joy knows no bounds. I pull her out of the chair, take her in my arms and dance a few steps to the closing strains of Guy Lombardo's "Enjoy Yourself" coming from the radio. Her soft cheek is close to mine and I'm in heaven.

"No wonder I love my little girl more than anything, and I mean anything, in the whole world."

The squeezing and kissing is progressing from cuddly to urgent. Blondie is a little short of breath. "Honey, do you want some more coffee?"

"Forget the coffee." I take a quick look at the kitchen clock which reads 11:52 PM. "It's still Saturday night and I have my beautiful wife. Come with me, little darlin'." I put my arm around her and lead her from the kitchen. She reaches out and shuts off the light. If the neighbors are looking, they can see us silhouetted as we kiss by the lamp in the living room. I pull the chain and we're surrounded by darkness as we make our way to paradise.

# CHAPTER TWENTY-FIVE

BLONDIE IS DRESSED FOR CHURCH AND SHE'S TRYING TO GET the kids to finish breakfast, so they won't be late for Sunday School. It's tough, but she's winning the battle. Coming down the stairs, I hear Larry ask, "Where's Dad?"

He doesn't have to wait for his answer—I entered the arch that leads to the kitchen.

"Your Dad's right here and your Dad has to get going."

Blondie gives me a knowing smile from the range where she's getting ready to break a couple of eggs into the frying pan. "Bulldog, I think you probably need a good breakfast to rebuild your energy. What would you like with your eggs?"

I come up behind her, take her in my arms, and plant a big kiss on her cheek. "No time, sweetheart. I want to get down to Desert Star Motors. You have my eggs, and then take the kids to church. I'll catch up with you at your mother's this afternoon."

I can see the disappointment in her eyes and I start to say something when the phone rings. Blondie picks it up with lightning speed. "Hi, Jim. No, he's here. He was just going out the door. Hold on. Detective James H. Vail, Phoenix Police Department for the famous Bulldog McLain."

If Jim is calling me at home, something hot is going down.

"Hi, Jim. What's up?" I pull the pad and pencil we always keep near the phone to write down the details. "I was just leaving to run down a lead on the missing person's case, but I'll change directions and meet you at the crime scene."

Blondie is busy scrambling her eggs, so I hug her from behind and whisper the news in her ear. "Jim has a homicide. There's a murder down behind the Bucket of Blood. My camera is in the car, so I'll be on my way. See you and the kids this afternoon."

We share a quick kiss and I'm out the door.

# CHAPTER TWENTY-SIX

I PULL UP BESIDE TWO PATROL CARS AND AN AMBULANCE PARKED on a side street that borders the Bucket of Blood, a dump on Phoenix's tough south side. The blinking lights on both police cars and the ambulance are like invitations to the area. A couple of uniformed officers have their hands full keeping the one hundred percent Hispanic on-lookers on the far side of the street. The morning dew is still on the field of weeds that stretches behind the club. I pick my way through this jungle, camera in hand. I manage to soak my socks, shoes, and the lower third of my pants before I join big, good-looking Detective Lieutenant Jim Vail.

"What have we got, Jim?"

"Murder One. Come over here."

He leads me through more wet weeds until we come upon the body of an elderly man lying on top of a pile of cardboard boxes. I unlimber the camera and start getting my pictures while making comments. "His throat is cut from ear to ear. The area looks as though he might have put up a fight."

"No matter how you slice it, Gene, it looks as though another old tramp has met a bad end."

I bend down by the body and finger the old man's sport

jacket. "Jim, I'm not so certain he was poor. This is a high quality coat and look at the shoes—they're expensive and, by the looks of the soles, they're pretty new. Did anybody see what happened?"

"Yeah, we have a witness. Detective Grasser took him downtown. I don't have to tell you that any eyeball witness in this area won't stay alive long if he fingers somebody. Grab your wheels and meet me at headquarters. Maybe you can get some kind of an angle for your story."

I get my car and drive out of the area. I slow down as I pass St. Mary's Catholic Church. The faithful are coming out of early mass not paying too much attention as to where they cross the street. Out of the corner of my eye I see Largo Sanchez, a tough punk with a long rap sheet. He seems to be in an argument with an older lady who I take to be his mother. She's pointing to the left sleeve of his white shirt that has something all over it. He says some angry words in Spanish and moves down the street as I work my way to the courthouse.

I ask the jailer on duty where they are holding the suspect and he directs me to one of the basement interrogation rooms.

As I push open the door, I'm greeted by Detective George Grasser, 5' 8", nice looking and immaculate as always in a light tan suit. Detective Grasser is one of the deadliest shots on the Phoenix Police force, as many criminals have found out too late. After a brief hello, Grasser turns his attention to Detective Bob Corrigan, who is working the suspect.

Corrigan, about 5'9" with dark wavy hair that has just a strand or two of silver showing, has removed his jacket. and his shoulder holster is empty. This is one tough cop who does not have a single shred of compassion for punks. He leans on the edge of the battered table over which a single light bulb dangles. Seated at the table in a heavy, splintered oak chair is a twenty-six year old Mexican-American named Jose Quintero.

I know this punk by sight and I'm not surprised to find him at the center of the detective's attention. His shifty eyes whip around the room—he's very nervous.

Detective Vail, who had been upstairs, enters the room, and Quintero gives a nervous twist in his chair. Vail remains in the shadows at the back of the small room with several other officers. I had better find out the ground rules of this little meeting.

"Detective Corrigan, what do we have here?"

Corrigan turns half around to see who is speaking, then turns back to Quintero. "Gene, what we have is a scumbag who was an eyeball witness to a murder, who is trying to act dumber than he is. In fact, he's trying to be very cute. I'm just about ready to show him what cute really is with a little 'one on one'."

Grasser's soft voice interrupts. "Jose, we're convinced that you know who the perp is." Quintero doesn't answer but shakes his head a couple of times.

I had to get into the act. "What's the story, George?"

"Gene, I don't know if you know this kind soul. His name is Jose Quintero. Our friend Jose has a nice fat rap sheet that includes assault with a deadly weapon, attempted murder and …"

Corrigan, who had been glaring at Jose, enters the conversation. "Don't forget, I brought this punk in two years ago on a rape charge. This guy's a real home boy."

Grasser turns to Quintero and in his soft voice says, "Jose, why don't you tell Mr. McLain what you told us?"

I focus hard on Quintero. Nervous twitches affect his scared and pock-marked face. He moves his shoulders with funny little jerky movements and his face is a mixture of hate and fear as he speaks in broken English.

"I'm coming up the street Mon, cutting through the lot behind the Bucket of Blood. Lots of tramps who drop off the trains sleep there and I thought …"

Grasser helps him along with his story.

"What he's trying to tell you is that he planned to roll the tramps for anything and everything they had—"

Corrigan takes over. "The problem is that a friend of his already had the action." Like a matador spinning away from a bull, Corrigan half-turns from Quintero and speaks over his shoulder. "Continue, Jose. McLain loves your story."

Raw hate fills Quintero's eyes as he looks at Corrigan. He meets the icy gaze of the veteran detective and his eyes lower. He clears his throat and continues.

"Hey, Mon, I don't roll no tramps. No stinking tramps for me. Anyone who says that I touch those bums is a liar."

This statement brings broken laughter from detective Vail and other officers standing in the shadows. Quintero tries to make out the faces beyond the single light, gives up, and moves on with his tale.

"Anyway, I'm coming up to the lot when I see a guy standing over an old tramp who looks like he's asleep."

Corrigan's voice cuts through. "Tell me what this punk was wearing."

"Mon, I told you before. He had a white shirt and black pants." Quintero squirms around in his seat and acts like the story is over. Detective Grasser brings him back to reality.

"Jose, I want you to repeat the story you told us. I want McLain to hear the same garbage you threw in our face. Now, what did the punk do and say next?"

"He reached for a bottle of wine the old tramp had in his hand. When he grabbed at it, the old tramp woke up and pulled the bottle away."

Corrigan's eyes look like hot coals as he speaks to Quintero. "Go on, you scumbag, before I have to break your neck."

Jose gets the message and moves on with his version of the murder.

"The young guy called the old Gringo a bastardo and told him to give him the wine. The old man told him to go fuck himself. The next thing I saw was the young guy had a switch-blade and was after the old man who got to his feet and tried to run. The young guy grabbed him, bent him backwards and slit his throat. The old man made funny sounds and a lot of blood came out of his mouth. He dropped on a pile of old cardboard. The young guy laughed, wiped his blade on the old man's coat, then drank the whole bottle of wine without stopping. When he finished, he kicked the old man a couple of times and walked out of the lot."

Grasser takes a long look at Jose before speaking. "Tell me again. Did this guy still have the bottle with him when he left the lot and did he have any blood on his shirt or pants that you could see?"

"I told you, Mon, he took the bottle with him. He stopped just as he got to the street and found he had blood on one arm of his white shirt "

Corrigan is having a tough time watching Quintero who, the longer he talks, the more sure of himself he becomes, until he's giving out with a street smart attitude.

"So, Jose, you're telling me this guy looked at the blood on his shirt, cursed, and you just watched him walk away?"

Quintero looks up with a sneer. "Hey, Mon, what did you expect me to do?"

I half expect Corrigan to make the sneer permanent on Jose's face with an iron hard fist.

"You son-of-a-bitch. You know and I know that Largo Sanchez killed that old man."

"Yeah, Jose," Grasser interjected, "there's only one guy on the south side that scares the shit out of you and that's Largo Sanchez. That's why you're twisting and turning and lying through your teeth."

"Mon, I don't even know any Largo Sanchez."

Like a streak of lightning, Corrigan reaches across the table, grabs Quintero by the lapels and hauls him out of the chair. He holds him so close their faces almost touch. "You and Largo were in on the jewelry store heist five years ago. You do remember being sent down to the state pen for that, don't you?"

Quintero's eyes bug with fear. "I was framed, Mon. I was innocent. That's why they let me out of the pen early. I was framed and they didn't prove shit on Largo."

Corrigan throws Quintero back into his chair as Grasser picks up the interrogation. "Yeah punk, you were framed, all right. Maybe I'll have Detective Corrigan take you down to the little room at the end of the hall so you two can have a heart to heart talk. I guarantee you'll be willing to tell us your *real* life story after that little session."

I have enough material to write a few paragraphs on the old man's murder. I need to follow up on the information about the 1940 Ford, so I excuse myself.

I get four blocks away when I remember what I saw in front of St. Mary's this morning. I do one of my famous U-turns and set some kind of new speed record for a four block drive to get back to police headquarters. I hotfoot it to the basement and all eyes turn as I enter the interrogation room. It looks as though they are through. Quintero is sitting relaxed in the chair with a smirk on his face. Corrigan and Grasser look like two guys who had their hands on a big prize, but had lost it.

Corrigan is the first to speak. "Okay, Bulldog. What did you forget?"

Grasser looks around the floor. "I don't see any notes. You must be losing it."

"I'm losing it all right. I stood right here and listened to all the crap that was being told about the old man's murder and forgot something I saw on my way over here this morning."

Grasser laughs, "Okay, Gene. What did you see?"

"I was driving by St. Mary's. Mass was over and the street was full of people, so I had to slow down to a crawl. Over on one corner, I saw Largo Sanchez with a lady I would guess is his mother. He was dressed in a sparkling white shirt and black pants, but his mother was really laying into him because he had stains of some kind all over the left forearm of his white shirt. Anyway, that's what I forgot."

As the door closes, I can see Grasser's face grow grim and Corrigan is clenching and unclenching his big fists. The last thing I remember is the stark fear on Quintero's face. I'm not sure, but as I start to exit to the parking lot, I can hear a thud and the splintering of a heavy oak chair.

# CHAPTER TWENTY-SEVEN

As I drive to Desert Star Used Cars, I find it hard to believe that it's only 10:15 on this beautiful Sunday morning.

Arriving at my destination, I find metal gates drawn across the entrance to a small lot that holds maybe twenty cars. There is a little building about as large as an old country outhouse that passes for the office. A note in the corner of the gate informs me that the owner of Desert Star Used Autos, one J.W. Benjamin, Jr., lives in the house that adjoins the lot on the east side.

The doorbell is broken, so I go to work pounding on the frame of the screen door. In a few seconds, I hear an upstairs window open and a voice demanding, "What's going on?"

I back off the porch into what passes for a yard, then look up into the face of one J.W. "Benny" Benjamin. My pounding has awakened Mr. Benjamin from what he considers his well-earned, late Sunday morning snooze. His hair is sticking out at all angles and he's trying to open his eyes and see me in the glare of the sun.

"Whatta you want? You crazy or something?"

"I'm Gene McLain from the *Arizona Reporter,* and I need to ask you a couple of questions about a car you sold."

"Look, fella, the lot opens at noon on Sunday. You come back then and we can have a long talk."

"I can't wait, Mr. Benjamin. I'm dealing with a case of double homicide."

I can tell by the way Mr. Benjamin shakes his head that he can't believe his ears. "Did you say homicide? You mean murder. Get in the shade on the porch. I'll be down in just a couple of minutes."

Benny, as I have been instructed to call him, unlocks the metal gate and slides it open. We stroll into his domain. A key on his big, old fashioned key ring works its magic on a padlock that holds his office door shut. To say that two people fill his little space is putting it mildly. I step back outside and wait for Benny to bring out a couple of manila envelopes that pass for a filing system. He lays the envelopes up on a little shelf that protrudes from his "office" and digs a pair of reading glasses out of his shirt pocket. He pops them over his ample nose, then opens the envelopes.

What a clutter of bills, receipts, notes and maybe even a recipe or two. But no matter how muddled it looks to me, Benny knows just where to find things. With a flourish, he withdraws a long bill of sale. "Ha, here it is. It was a 1940 Ford. I sold it to one Charlie Andrews. He lives in Los Angeles, California, at a place called the Hotel Cecil located on Main Street in that fair 'City of the Angels.'"

He hands the piece of paper to me and I read the details.

"Mr. Benjamin, this is very interesting. This fellow Andrews purchased this car the day *before* another auto salesman and his client vanished. By the way you act, I would guess that you have a very vivid memory regarding this sale. Why?"

"Of course I remember this deal. This fellow Andrews paid cash. Now I ask you, how many people ever buy a car and pay cash? Certified checks, personal checks, but almost never do they pay cash. Also, he didn't take delivery of the car until the following afternoon."

"Let me be certain I have this right. He bought the car on Friday and paid you cold, hard cash, but he left the car here on the lot and didn't pick it up until the next day which would have been Saturday afternoon. That's the same day the auto salesman and his client vanished."

"You've got it right. That's just the way it happened."

"Mr. Benjamin, what do you remember about Charlie Andrews?"

"You mean outside of the fact that he paid cash? Well, he's a real good looking kid, you know, the kind the girls are crazy about. You might say that he's the All-American boy. He has dark curly hair, he's tall and slender, and he has a million dollar smile. I remember, I told him he should be in sales. Believe me, he could sell all the ladies."

I can already picture Benjamin as an important witness for the D.A., so I press on.

"Do you remember anything else? Anything you might not have told me?"

"No, Mr. McLain, I don't think so. Oh, yeah—he's left handed. He had a little trouble signing the sales slip up here on my small shelf."

# CHAPTER TWENTY-EIGHT

NOW I HAVE A NAME OUT OF THE BLUE. SOMEONE CALLED Charlie Andrews, and I have Mr. Benjamin keeping a sales slip for a 1940 Ford under lock and key until we can see if this leads anywhere. There's no use in trying to find out anything more about Harold Severson. He's new in town, hasn't had time to make friends and establish regular places where he eats or shops, plus he spends most of his off hours with his mother, but George Williams is another story. The obvious thing is to find Williams or someone who knows where he went, or what his plans were before he disappeared. With this in mind, I find myself standing in front of the Williams residence.

The wind chimes are still tinkling. As I get to the front porch, I can hear Bing Crosby and his son, Gary, doing their swinging version of the current hit, "Sam's Song," from a radio deep inside the house. As before, the bell fails to produce anyone, but my fist against the frame of the screen door gets attention. The sexy Mrs. Williams appears in a very short silk smock that leaves little to the imagination. Her magnificent breasts are two-thirds exposed, and from the gap in her brief silk jacket, her thick pubic patch provides solid evidence that she's a natural blonde. Her hair is tousled and I have a distinct feeling that this lady has just returned from a trip, or had a long and active night on the town. The ever-present cigarette dangles from her ruby red lips and the beautiful green eyes have that old flicker of suspicion working overtime. She opens the screen door and leans against the frame.

"So, you're back again. What the hell do you want? Don't you know it's Sunday?"

"Yes, Mrs. Williams, I am very much aware that today is Sunday, but I'm still trying to locate your husband. Have you heard anything from him?"

She pulls the cigarette from between her soft lips and exhales a cloud of smoke into my face.

"I told you before and I'll tell you one more time. When he gets back, he gets back. And, Mr. Reporter, when he does get back, I'll have him give you a fat lip if you don't quit bothering me."

She puts the cigarette back in her mouth and gives me that up and down stud evaluation as before. It's obvious I fail the test.

"Look, Sonny, don't come around again asking your stupid questions."

As she blows a cloud of smoke in my face, I look past one of her shapely legs and see a suitcase sitting in the hall. I put two and two together. It's time to let her know that although she's pretty smooth, she can't pull the wool over the Bulldog's eyes. I take my shot.

"I guess it gets pretty tiring making regular trips to Las Vegas. But I suppose Johnny Saita's worth it."

She gives the screen door a vicious slam, but it springs open as she turns away. I wonder how many men have been driven to distraction by her hip movement that invokes the wildest desires. The fact that her smock fails to cover the bottom of her creamy white buttocks adds to the picture as she disappears within the darkened house as Perry Como sings "Hoop-Dee-Doo."

# CHAPTER TWENTY-NINE

VISITING THE SEVERSON HOME THIS SUNDAY AFTERNOON WILL be a tough waste of time, but I feel it's my duty to check on the lady and, of course, there is always the outside chance that I can pick up on something to break the log jam. The immaculate lawn at Winter Garden Manor is getting the water treatment from a series of sprinklers that spray out lazy arcs of the life-giving liquid. I knock at the Severson unit and the door is opened by a middle aged lady who, from Blondie's description, has to be the nurse and house-keeper, Iva Roper.

"I'm Gene McLain of the *Arizona Reporter* and I would guess that you are Mrs. Roper. I would like to have a few words with Mrs. Severson, if possible."

Mrs. Roper eyes me in a friendly way before she speaks. "Mrs. Severson has been placed under a doctor's care. He is very concerned about what all this trauma will do in her frail condition. I do know that she would like to see you, but you must be brief."

I agree to a very short stay. Mrs. Roper leads me to a back bedroom. The shades are drawn against the afternoon heat and the swamp cooler makes the room comfortable. Mrs. Severson, looking gaunt and frail, is propped up by several fat pillows. I'm surprised how far downhill she has gone since I saw her last.

"Mr. McLain, I'm afraid that something terrible has happened to my son. He's vanished, just vanished."

"Mrs. Severson, we can only hope for the best."

I hand her the envelope that encloses the photo of Harold that she had provided. "This is your photo of Harold. It's as good as new. I hope that Harold will soon be returning. We do know that Mr. Williams is still missing. His wife, and everyone else I have talked to—and believe me, I have talked with people from one end of town to the other—all think your son and Mr. Williams are in Mexico. Also, though it took them forever, the police have listed your son as a missing person."

Her eyes blaze with a strange light as she leans forward and puts every ounce of her strength into what she says.

"I can't believe that story, Mr. McLain, and I don't think you believe it either. Do you know what I think? I think my son has been *murdered!*"

The air is charged with electricity. For a moment, the lady sits straight up in bed. Then, like a balloon with the air released, she collapses in slow motion back onto her stack of pillows and closes her eyes.

Making my way out to the front, I thank Mrs. Roper, and leave this place of sorrow.

# CHAPTER THIRTY

I ROLL DOWN THE WINDOWS IN THIS SWEATBOX OF A CAR AND review what I have learned to date. With the exception of Mrs. Severson and myself, everyone thinks George Williams, Harold Severson, and their client are somewhere in Mexico. George Williams, whom a million people seem to know, has been the thread running through my investigation. With one exception, I have visited every single place that George has been known to spend a lot of time at. I start the engine and head down Central Avenue toward the last possible place I might find a contact who can tell me where the elusive Mr. Williams has gone.

Gazarra's Gym may not be as well-known as the famous Main Street Gym in Los Angeles, or several of the gyms in New York that are used by the major professional boxers, but Gazarra's offers plenty of action: this afternoon is no exception. In fact, I have a hard time finding a parking place. I'm wondering *why all the extra activity*, until I remember that a local boy, Jimmy

Martinez, is in the final week of training before a big fight in New York that could put him in line for a shot at a world title.

Jimmy, a handsome Mexican-American, is one of the hottest items in professional boxing today. He's had some great showcases on the nationally televised Friday Night Fights. A good puncher, his fame rests on his superb boxing ability. Those handsome features don't have a mark on them and that's because Jimmy only gives hits, he doesn't get hit.

If you've ever spent time in the rooms where fighters toil, you'll recognize the smells of sweat, blood, liniment and leather mixed together, and you'll never forget it. Add to that the smoke from cigarettes and cigars that hangs over every-thing like a foggy cloud, and you have the picture. It always amazes me that fighters train in this kind of atmosphere. I guess if the smoke doesn't kill you, that means you'll have a good shot at surviving an opponent.

The big crowd is around the center ring where Jimmy, head guard in place and sweat covering his handsome features, is giving his sparring partner a lesson in the sweet science. I watch a round or two and start to move away. As I turn, I run into a guy I have known for years. One of the greatest middleweight champions who ever lived, none other than Lou Ambers, the battler who came out of Herkimer, New York, to become a legend in ring history. Lou was one of the few fighters who had an honest manager who invested his money so that, for the rest of his life, he can live comfortably. He gives me that lopsided smile and his beaten visage, full of scar tissue and cut lines, lights up like a Christmas tree. We shake hands and I guide Lou to a back wall.

"Hey, Champ, you're looking great. How do you think our boy Jimmy is going to do next week when he's back in the Big Apple?"

"No sweat, Gene. Unless the roof of Madison Square Garden falls in on him, Jimmy will win—an easy decision. He's got to be the best boxer in the game today."

"Lou, away from the fight game, by any chance have you

seen George Williams? Do you happen to know where he might be?"

"Gosh, Gene, George has to be in Mexico, because I haven't seen him for a long time. He comes here, oh, maybe three days a week to work out. George always keeps in shape. He has to, with all the broads who make demands on his time and energy."

Lou laughs and so do I. George has some kind of reputation. Tough guy, lady killer, and top salesman.

"Lou, I'm gonna get going, but just in case you see George, would you give me a ring over at the paper? I really need to get in touch with him."

"Sure thing, Gene. Hey, I wish you'd stick around. Jimmy's going to work one more sparring partner. This is the last time we'll see him until after the big fight."

"Lou, I'd love to, but remember, I'm not retired and I've got a beautiful wife and a couple of great kids to feed."

Lou moves back into the crowd around ringside and I start toward the front door. There are several pugs shadow boxing, making music on the speed bag or skipping rope. What catches my attention is the flashy middleweight over in a corner who is showing a lot of moves as he whacks a big bag. The guy's back looks familiar, but I don't put the name and the body together until he steps back and gives the bag a rest. I say hello to Detective Lou Steinberg who, for my dough, is a real story with the Phoenix PD.

Lou was born in Tennessee where he excelled in high school as a straight A student, plus he had a well-earned reputation as a top Golden Gloves boxer. He had offers to turn pro, but Lou always had a great deal of ambition to make something of himself in another career, one with a long life. Lou is not only one of the most likeable guys I have ever known, but he's loaded with chutzpa and savvy. He knocked them dead in college where he majored in Criminal Justice. During a vacation break, he met a pretty girl. They fell in love, got married, and decided they would like to live where the summer spends the winter. Lou graduated from the Police Academy with top honors and made detective in record time. He and his wife have three children. At present, he's attending night law school with the goal of being a top notch attorney. A couple more years and he will be giving the DA fits as a member of his staff, pressing for the top spot in the department, or as a defense attorney sitting across the courtroom ready to do battle.

I stop and chat with Lou, who is interested in my progress on the missing persons case. I bring him up to date on the murder this morning at the Bucket of Blood. After we talk, he heads to the shower, then home. The family's going to barbecue and it'll be fun being with his wife and kids. Later in the evening, he will spend two or three hours hitting the law books for his Monday night class.

Driving home, I realize that I have just about exhausted any leads on George Williams. All I have is the name of a Charlie Andrews who bought a 1940 Ford the day before the salesmen vanished. The odds are heavy that his old Ford can be tied to a case fast disappearing in the mists of time that involves a new car. According to Specs, the DA, and the police department, this old car has nothing to do with anything or anyone. If I was someone else, I'd move on to something new, but then, that's why they call me "Bulldog." Before I go home, I'm going to take some drastic steps to get this case back in the headlines on a national basis.

# CHAPTER THIRTY-ONE

I ARRIVE AT THE *REPORTER* AROUND 6:00 PM. THERE'S NO one in the place, so the phones are silent. I spend a few minutes sitting in front of my beat-up standard Royal typewriter. I insert a clean sheet of paper and start pounding out my story with two fingers. You can laugh if you want to, but I can write faster with two fingers than any secretary working at this paper can with ten.

At last, I rip the final page of my story out of the carriage, pick up my other sheets of the copy, plus a couple of photographs laying face down on my desk. I head downstairs to the composing room.

Here, in the vast area that contains the presses, I find my old friend Ben Berger wearing, as always, his clean bib overalls and a plaid shirt. I hand him the sheets with my layout and story, along with the photographs.

"Ben, be certain that this goes on the front page of tomorrow's *Reporter* and see that it goes out on the AP wire for syndication."

Old Ben has a big smile lighting his wrinkled, suntanned face. "Have we got another award winner?"

"I don't know about awards, Ben, but it will sure get Specs' attention."

"By the way, Gene, Specs didn't tell me this priority was coming down. I'll have to move some stories around."

"Ben, you know as well as I do that would-be reporters who become editors sometimes get behind on things. I can guarantee you that Specs loves this one."

I run up the stairs to my desk and make a quick call to Detective Vail at his residence. "I know, you want to know why I'm calling you at home on a Sunday night. I love to keep in touch with all you valiant police officers. You guys know where the action's at."

Jim tells me Quintero is back on the streets. They couldn't hold him. They brought Largo Sanchez in, but the white shirt in question was missing and Quintero couldn't identify Largo as the old man's killer. Jim also informed me that Quintero left headquarters with a broken nose. Detective Corrigan said Jose fell down the stairs, and if the detective said so, I'm sure that's what happened.

I have to ask about the missing person's case. Jim informs me that Deputy Morse said for everyone to forget about it, because there is no case. So, there's no case. Well, we'll see what tomorrow brings.

# CHAPTER THIRTY-TWO

I GET HOME MINUTES BEFORE BLONDIE. I FIX SOME GRILLED cheese sandwiches, a salad, and ice tea while Blondie changes into her robe. She joins me and I tell her that the possible Broaddus-Williams insurance tie-in is out the window. Otherwise, I keep the talk away from work until we finish dinner.

I can't hide it any longer. I tell Blondie the radical step I have taken to establish that this is a major case of homicide. I want to force a break that can bring about the capture of the killer and bring the case to a conclusion.

Blondie looks as though she has been hit with a sledge hammer. "You did what?"

I explain again how I wrote a feature story, both for local consumption and for national syndication. It will run under the photographs of George Williams and Harold Severson, and above the photos will be a blazing headline that will scream:

## "WHERE ARE THESE MURDERED MEN?"

I'm pacing the floor, trying to make my point. "Look honey, I have to bring this to a head and the only way I can do it is to use the most powerful tool that has ever been invented. The power of the press."

"Gene, you've lost it. You have to be crazy. This move will cost you your career. We'll lose our home, and think about the children."

I stop in front of my bride and give my best sales pitch. "Believe me, I thought it all through. Blondie, you know I'm a homicide reporter, that's all I've ever wanted to be and I'm damn good at my job. I know homicide and I'm telling you that what we have here is a double murder. I know it. I feel it. I can almost taste it."

The tears are rolling down her cheeks. Then, she stands and puts her arms around my neck. "Gene, I love you no matter what. Your family loves you, but you're driving me crazy. That story is going to put a lot of strain on your family and, let's be honest, it could destroy everything we've worked for."

I stroke her hair and hold her tight.

"Honey, what you're saying is true, but I have to do what I have to do. Just believe me that if everything comes crashing down, someway, somehow I'll take care of you and the kids."

She looks up smiling with her eyes filled with tears. "Bulldog, I'm with you all the way. I guess that's one of the reasons I've always loved you so much. You believe in yourself and, honey, you're the best, the very best."

My lips find hers and her kisses take me to paradise. Through the years, when things have been the roughest, Blondie's kiss has made everything better. She pulls a hanky out of the pocket of her robe and wipes her eyes.

"Now, tell me again, McLain: what does your story say?"

# CHAPTER THIRTY-THREE

LAYING ACROSS THE DESK IS THE FRONT PAGE OF THIS morning's paper. Big black headlines ask the question, **"WHERE ARE THESE MURDERED MEN?"** Under the headline are photos of a grim looking George Williams and a smiling Harold Severson. Then the byline, story by Gene McLain.

The paper in question covers the desk of Editor Ralph "Specs" Bornheim, who pounds the paper as if to destroy it. I feel he's getting near the red alert of a heart attack when he points at me and screams. "How in the hell did you ever get this printed? Not only in Arizona but on the national wire to boot? There is *no* proof that these men have been murdered. In fact, our police say that they have grave doubts that these men are even missing persons. You are so very sure of yourself. I want to know where these men are and I want to know now!"

Specs' secretary, Jan Kerr, enters. "Mr. Bornheim, Mr. Sacks, our publisher, is on the line."

Specs does a 360 degree turnaround. He grabs up the phone and starts to fawn. I watch him shifting from foot to foot hoping the finger of guilt will not be pointing at him. I'm only privy to his side of the conversation, but I'm sure I'm not too far off on what the Sacks is saying.

"Yes sir, I can assure you that I had no knowledge that this story was in our paper, let alone in national syndication. Yes, sir, I agree. McLain must have told the composing room that the story had my okay. Yes, sir, he's here in my office. I'll put him on." Specs jams his finger at me and hands me the phone. The next sound I hear is that of David V. Sacks, owner and publisher, who's voice level is just one degree below screaming.

"You're through, McLain. Through with this paper, through with any paper. The *Reporter* will be sued. The Associated Press will be sued and your bungling will make me the laughing stock of the publishing world. My standing as a national figure will be damaged beyond repair. Do you have even the slightest idea of what you have done? You and your vivid imagination that these men are dead?"

Specs is standing behind the desk gloating, but I don't think I've batted an eyelash, so when Sacks pauses for breath, I speak.

"Sir, I'm telling you, these men are dead. This is a first class case of Murder One. There is *no* doubt in my mind about this. This is a homicide, a double homicide."

All is still for a heartbeat. The publisher, whose rage is now under control, starts spinning a web that could lead to my destruction. "McLain, you're nothing but a hot-shot who got lucky and won a couple of awards. Bornheim should throw you out the front door. I'm an international figure and around the world I'm known as a compassionate man, one who believes in the goodness of his fellow man. Being that kind of a person, I am going to give you a chance, a chance you don't deserve."

He gives a dramatic pause and I wait for the jaws of the trap to snap shut.

"You're so cocky and certain that this is a homicide case, so I'm going to give you the benefit of the doubt. Because I believe in my fellow man, I'm going to give you forty-eight hours from right now to come up with the bodies. Should you fail to do what an entire police department has failed to do, there will be no town small enough for you to find work as a reporter. By the way, McLain, anything, and I mean *anything*, you write during this next forty-eight hours *will* be cleared by Bornheim. Put him back on the line."

He repeats our, or rather his, conversation to Bornheim. The smirk on Specs' face is a yard wide and I am considering the idea that I should wipe it off, but at the last second I remember he is the Editor.

"Well, McLain, you heard the ultimatum. You have forty-eight hours, no more, no less, and then you're out of here. Just so you are aware"—he indicates a guy with slick hair and a thin mustache who had entered while the Sacks was on the phone—"I have hired 'Skull' Wright, a top homicide reporter from Chicago, who will take over this supposed case when the allotted forty-eight hours are over."

Wright looks at me buffing his nails as he speaks. "Yeah, McLain, you don't know how they do things in the big town. This is a simple missing person's case and I'll work with the cops and—"

Smacking the Editor is one thing, but I've had enough of this character. I drive forward and slam him into the wall. For a second, I think he's going to drop dead with a heart attack from pure fright. I put my face against his and let the spittle fly.

"Listen punk. Stay off my beat and off my case. If I catch you at the courthouse, you won't be able to hide behind Specs' skirts."

Bornheim, who has been frozen as the action takes place, recovers, scurries around the desk, and steps in front of Skull to protect him.

"Just a minute, McLain. I'll have none of your Irish hooligan tactics in my office."

I pause for a couple of heartbeats to let the anger die, then head for the exit. Before leaving, I give them one parting shot. "You two great reporters deserve each other." I slam the door so hard it sounds like a cannon firing. All heads jerk up at the reporters' desks as I head down the stairs toward the courthouse.

# CHAPTER THIRTY-FOUR

MORSE'S OFFICE IS EMPTY. I HELP MYSELF TO A CUP OF steaming coffee just as Harry and the DA come through the door. O'Neill can hardly wait to start his speech.

"Well, you really made a fool of yourself this time, printing a story without a shred of truth. Don't you understand that if a crime has occurred, I would release the bloodhounds and solve the case? But of course, no crime has been committed. This really blows your reporter's intuition theory into a cocked hat."

"Mr. O'Neill, I know you're a college man and a majority of our citizens elected you to bring a stop to crime in this city, but I believe we are dealing with a case of double homicide. And yes, my reporter's intuition tells me this is true. I'm at a point where I can do one of four things. I can put the pieces of this puzzle together and find the murdered men; I can quit the paper, sell our house and take Blondie and the kids away from all this craziness, but I have no intention of doing that; I can stand here and go quietly out of my mind; or, I can get Deputy Morse to call the Hotel Cecil in Los Angeles to check out if Charlie Andrews is currently living there or if he has ever been a resident of that hotel."

Harry looks at me like he has never seen me before and isn't sure he ever wants to see me again. "Forget it, Gene. There is no way I am going to try and tie the disappearance of Williams and Severson to a ten year-old abandoned car. Just forget it. It's not going to happen."

# CHAPTER THIRTY-FIVE

I TAKE THE ELEVATOR DOWN TO THE PRESS ROOM IN THE
basement and make my call. I get the desk clerk at the Hotel
Cecil in Los Angeles who speaks to me off and on throughout
at least fifty interruptions. This guy gives me a song and
dance that he is overworked and underpaid. I ask him if he
will call me at the *Reporter* in three hours to let me know what
he has found out about Charlie Andrews. I check my watch
and realize that I have just fifteen minutes before I meet
Blondie for lunch at the Eagle. I stop by the bank and cash
my check, then put the bulk of it in our joint savings account.
I wonder if I will ever be getting another paycheck from the
*Reporter*.

When I arrive at the Eagle, the word is out on the street.
Mary Olive, the boss lady, doesn't quite meet my eyes when
she greets me and even Jo Oakes, Arizona's prettiest waitress,
acts like she is serving guests at a wake. As I slide in the booth
opposite Blondie, she addresses the issue at hand. "The scut-
tlebutt around the courthouse is that your career with the
*Reporter* will be finished in a week."

I give her my best Humphrey Bogart look, but it isn't
working. "Sweetheart, you don't really think that David V.

Sacks would grant me an entire week to wrap up my career, do you?"

Blondie turns pale and for the first time ever I can see she's scared. "How long?"

"Forty-eight hours."


Back at the *Reporter*, my lunch feels like lead in my stomach. I know that Blondie, at the department office, is worried sick. I wait and wait for the LA call. Meanwhile, I notice that the other reporters are sneaking sly glances my way when they think they won't be caught. I guess it's just natural to want to look at the condemned man.

Bornheim and Skull Wright come onto the floor and go into Specs' office. The way they're chatting away makes me think that Specs popped for lunch at The Flame and the two of them are planning great events in the art of homicide reporting.

The phone jangling snaps me back as the operator informs me I have a collect call from Los Angeles. It is my main man in the field or, rather, my man at the desk of the Hotel Cecil.

He gives me the bad news that he has gone through the current register and that Charlie Andrews is not now a guest at the Hotel Cecil, nor has he been a guest during the term of this register. I ask him about older registers and he informs me with a vocal sneer that they keep them for a period of years and they are thrown in a bin down in the basement. He repeats that he is overworked and underpaid. Thinking he would like to pick up some extra cash, I offer to pay him if he will go through the registers during his time off to see if he can locate when and if Charlie Andrews was around. He tells me what I can do with my money and slams down the phone. So much for his help at any price.

I look up to find Tommy Seymour, one of our office boys,

standing by my desk. "Souper," as we have nicknamed Tommy because of his love for "Chicken Pot," is looking at me with big eyes. I guess he also wants a closer look at the condemned.

"Mr. McLain, while you were on the phone, Detective James Vail called. He's at the morgue and would like for you to meet him there as soon as possible."

I jump to my feet. "Thanks, Tommy. I'm on my way."

# CHAPTER THIRTY-SIX

I SAY HELLO TO THE MORGUE ATTENDANTS AND FIND JIM IN A cold room standing beside a roll-out drawer that holds the mortal remains of the old man murdered behind the Bucket of Blood. The body has been cleaned and the old man, with his hair combed and the sheet pulled up to his chin, looks as though he is having a peaceful sleep.

"What's up, Jim? Something new on the old man?"

"Gene, I have to hand it to you. Your intuition was right on track. This old gentleman was certainly not your run of the mill bum. When we went through his clothes we found five thousand dollars sewed into the lining of his jacket. This should give you the base for a powerful human interest story, and if you can get it out on the AP wire, we might get lucky and get an identification."

"I'm going back to the *Reporter*. I'll knock out a few paragraphs. I know Specs will be happy the story is about a stiff who's in the morgue. I'll find a little different slant for the story, but sad to say, no matter how it goes, it won't have a happy ending."

I take my time walking back. I enjoy the afternoon

sunshine and think about the hundreds of times I have made this walk before. Now, it could be my last.

# CHAPTER THIRTY-SEVEN

THE STORY ON THE OLD MAN GOT SPECS' STAMP OF APPROVAL for both local and wire release. In fact, I see the start of the story on Page One as I pick up a copy of the *Reporter* from the boy selling papers in front of the courthouse the following morning. Specs is acting strange. I wonder, could Specs be thinking how lonesome it will be without his favorite reporter? My mind drifts off with that thought and I almost walk into Jim Vail up in the squad room. It's a good thing I missed him, since he's pouring a steaming cup of coffee. He hands the cup to me along with a fresh baked doughnut.

"What's the status with Sacks and the missing persons caper?"

"It's just wonderful. He gave me forty-eight hours to come up with the bodies. Since that instant, I haven't been able to generate a single lead and time's running out. In fact, as of this moment I have two hours and twelve minutes to do something."

Vail sits down at his desk and takes a big gulp of coffee before speaking. "Over the years, I've followed your career closely and you're one hell of a homicide reporter, there's no doubt about that. You also are the luckiest guy I've ever known. When crunch time comes up, you always seem to be in the right place at the right time."

"How do you figure that Jim?"

"Maybe it's the luck of the Irish, or maybe the man upstairs feels you're special."

"I'd like to have some of that luck now, before time runs out."

Detective Corrigan enters the squad room and makes for the coffee and doughnuts. This guy should own a doughnut shop—he loves 'em! "Hi, Gene, Jim. I have to have my java and a sinker before I can get it all together. Has anyone seen Palumbo?"

"Don't get in a sweat this early in the day. Joe called in about ten minutes ago. He has to get a prescription filled for his daughter. He said she was sick all night. Said to tell you he'd be here as soon as possible."

Corrigan has his mouth full of doughnut but answers anyway.

"That's good news. We're the number one catchers this morning and I really don't want to handle any of the city's problems without brother Joseph. Bulldog, what's the latest on the missing person's case?"

"Nothing—that's the problem. I'm gonna wander down the hall. Maybe heavenly deliverance will strike me?"

I walk out into the silent hall and get about halfway down to the stairs when I hear a phone ring. Corrigan calls out to me.

I do double time getting back to the squad room. I manage not to slop coffee all over my clothes, but I do leave a brown trail along the hall.

Jim holds out the phone to me. The man on the other end of the conversation wants to know if I'm McLain, the reporter. I tell him I am one and the same, and he in turn tells me that he is Domingo Bermudez. He says he likes my stories but he has to read them to the other members of his family, because he's the only one who reads English. I really am not in the mood for this kind of small talk and I'm looking for a way to say goodbye. By now, Vail is on his second cup of coffee and Corrigan is on his third doughnut. At last, I thank Mr. Bermudez for calling and am just about to hang up when he changes the tone of his voice. In no uncertain terms, he tells me that he is a sheepherder and that both he and his sheep are troubled. I try to explain that I don't know the first thing about herding sheep, and that I have to go! He reacts with greater passion. He tries to explain that the reason he and his sheep are disturbed is because of the story I have written about Severson and Williams. I'm ready to slam down the phone on this crackpot, but I try one more soothing line. I tell him that neither he nor his sheep should be disturbed by any story that I write. He says that they wouldn't be, except the sheep don't like the men's bodies on their grassy range.

The adrenalin shoots through me like a streak of lightning as I grab a pen and pad of paper off Vail's desk. Domingo, that dear soul, is certainly *not* a crackpot after all. He has told me where the bodies are located, on the South Mountain Range, and promises to wait for me at the old corral where the trails fork. From there, he will take me to the site of the murders.

I hang up and for a couple of seconds my chest hurts. I can't get a word out, and when McLain can't get a word out, you know he's in trouble.

Vail stands up to get a closer look. He thinks I'm sick. "What's up? Are you okay?"

"I've never been better in my life. Domingo Bermudez, God bless him, and his sheep. The sheep! They found the bodies. Look, I've got to get out of here and meet Domingo down by the old corral on the back side of South Mountain. Do me a favor: call Grasser and Morse and tell them I'll meet them at the forks and take them to the bodies. You had better call the meat wagon and alert Doc Pearis and his boys. Also, don't forget to call O'Neill."

I set a world record for the one hundred yard dash. I tear out the back door of the court house and streak into the parking lot. I startle the trustee who is the lot attendant. My heap is in the garage for needed repairs, but Blondie's car will do.

"Where's Blondie's car?"

The trustee looks at me as if he is dealing with a madman. "She took it about ten minutes ago. Said she was on assignment."

There is no time to fool around, so I sprint to the parking area where the city of Phoenix keeps their patrol cars. I jerk open the door of the nearest black and white and get behind the wheel. I slam the door and turn the waiting key in the ignition. The tires scream as I back out of the parking space, then reverse and head for the driveway. The trustee is trying to block my exit to the street. His arms are waving wildly and he's screaming.

"You can't take a police car! You can't take a police car!"

I lean out the now open driver's window and beckon him to come to me. He shuffles sideways with a crab like motion and takes special care not to get close enough to the door so that I can grab him. I give him my best McLain smile as I break the bad news. "Give Chief Bleiler my regards and tell him I said thanks."

I jam the gas pedal to the floor and careen into the empty street. Within seconds I have the lights flashing and the siren wailing. I'm on my way!

# CHAPTER THIRTY-EIGHT

---

DOMINGO BERMUDEZ MEETS ME ON THE FAR SIDE OF SOUTH Mountain by the old corral where the road forks. I leave the patrol car and walk with Domingo to where some of his sheep are waiting. Then we proceed along a hardly discernible path for about three hundred yards. He stops and points. Sure enough, there, face down in an arroyo, are the decomposing bodies of two men. We're careful not to touch anything close to the crime scene and walk back down to where I left the black and white.

The first arrival is Detective Steinberg. He brings a uniformed officer with him to take my "borrowed" car back to headquarters. It is evident that the method of transportation I had selected is already history and Lou, being the thoughtful and caring guy he is, wants to minimize the damage by getting the car back in the motor pool as fast as possible.

Within fifteen minutes everything is strictly routine. The area is marked off. Lou and another officer find some tire tracks that could belong to the killer's car and they have been sealed off waiting for the lab boys to arrive. Here, inside the main yellow markers, we have Dr. Pearis, the County Medical Examiner, and his assistants. Doc Pearis, a slow talking, articulate native of West Virginia is, for my money, the best Medical Examiner in the whole USA. Detective George Grasser is in charge with Lou as his assistant. A very quiet Deputy Morse and the District Attorney have just arrived, making up the "in" group. Outside the crime scene four uniformed officers are keeping a small crowd of Hispanic on-lookers away. Grasser sets the crime scene.

"They were shot from behind, execution style. I'm certain, after checking the wounds, that the killer used a .45 automatic. Their hands are wired behind their backs and each victim was dispatched with a single shot to the head."

Detective Steinberg kneels by the heads of the victims. "From the angle that the bullets entered, I would say that the gun was fired by a left handed shooter."

The DA seems irritated that yours truly has found the bodies and is not doing a good job of hiding his displeasure. "Are we one hundred percent certain that these bodies are the missing salesmen?"

Grasser turns to Doc Pearis and his crew. "Roll 'em over, Doc."

Doc Pearis, who has to have one of the worst jobs in the world, always treats a corpse like he's handling a baby. No rough stuff like I have seen with coroners or medical examiners in other places. He pushes up his glasses, motions to his boys and, gently, they turn the bodies over.

As you might expect, the ants and other desert creatures have been having a feast since the day of the murders. Parts of both wide-eyed faces have been eaten away and the ants are running in and out of eye sockets, ears and nostrils. The bodies give off that awful odor of putrefying flesh, but even in this condition there is no doubt about the identity of the victims. I'm quick to point this out to the DA who is covering his handsome face with a white handkerchief and looking green around the gills.

"How about that, Counselor, Williams and Severson.

Murder One, just as I told you. Hey, Doc, when do you plan to do the autopsy?"

"Gene, we'll be doing it early this afternoon. This is a priority case."

The DA is flushed and more than half sick with the stench from the bodies. I can tell by his walk that he is very angry, as he moves to the far side of the crime scene. He indicates that I should join him.

"Well, McLain, you really got lucky and I mean real lucky. Don't ever try a stunt like you pulled in the newspapers again, because you'll never in this world be this lucky, not ever."

You know me, I couldn't let O'Neill have the last word. "There was no luck involved, Counselor. Just good investigative reporting by someone who has spent the best part of his life on the homicide beat."

As I'm giving O'Neill my thought for the day, the meat wagon arrives with the siren wailing, although the need for a siren has passed weeks ago. Right behind them comes KPHO-TV with their film gear and reporter Jack Murphy leading the charge. Cars from KOOL, KOY, and KTAR Radio follow: the race is on. Before the storm hits, I have one more chance to have a bit of a word with the District Attorney. I give him my best Irish brogue.

"Ah, Mr. O'Neill, faith and begorrah, here comes the wee television and radio folk with a chance for you to build on your future campaign to become governor of this great state. I know all the fairy folk can't wait to talk with you to find out just how you located the bodies of those poor dead laddies over there in the ditch."

The glare from the DA's eyes could melt steel, but only for an instant. He recovers his political self and turns toward the reporters bearing down on him with his famous smile. "Right this way, gentlemen. Right this way."

# CHAPTER THIRTY-NINE

THE SUMMER STORM CLOUDS THAT HAVE BEEN MOVING TOWARD the city all afternoon have let go and the rain is falling in torrents. What a delightful evening to be home. The kids are playing in the living room while Blondie and I talk over a cup of coffee.

"I don't know about you, Gene, but I'm very happy because our lives can go back to normal. The tension these past few days has been unbearable. Everyone gives me sad looks and I can't begin to count how many people came up and told me they knew what I was going through and wished us luck."

"I'm glad it's over too. However, I still have a major problem. Down at headquarters they're mumbling that this is a perfect crime. No motive and no indication who the killer or killers could be. They're talking about putting a couple of detectives on the case. They'll try and check everything about William's and Severson's backgrounds to see if they can dig up any enemies who would have had a reason to kill them."

"Gene, you've got to be kidding. You're telling me that they think this is some kind of a revenge killing?"

"That's what they're saying, but you and I both know it's

hogwash. They will spend endless hours and money following leads that will take them nowhere. I asked Harry once again to at least think about a tie-in with the 1940 Ford. He exploded, so that's a dead issue. I asked Specs for the time and expense money to go to Los Angeles to follow the Charlie Andrews angle. He said I could take a couple days off and go, but no expense money, and I can't afford to do that. No matter how much I try to change my own mind I can't lose the nagging feeling that the final answer to this case is somewhere in those hotel records."

A flash of lightning lights up the kitchen. The lights in the house dim, then come back up. The kids give a whoop and holler thinking this is great fun and squint out the rain covered front windows to see if lightning might skip across the tops of the mountains like it sometimes does.

Blondie gives me an intent look after my statement regarding the hotel records. She stands and looks me dead in the eye. "You just can't let this thing go, can you?" She walks over to the cupboard and rummages in the back, then pulls out an old cookie jar that we haven't used since the kids were born. She sets it on the table, opens the lid, then pushes it toward me.

"Gene, I bet you forgot about this. When we were first married, we promised each other that someday we would have a real honeymoon. Maybe Hawaii or Bermuda. There was a time when both of us used to drop coins or bills in this jar for our magical trip. After a while, I think you just forgot, but from time to time I've slipped a dollar or two into the fund. Right now, a real honeymoon doesn't seem as important as your solving this case. If Specs will okay the time off like he told you he would, I want you to take this money, go to Los Angeles, and wrap this story up once and for all."

What have I ever done to deserve a wife like this? How can one guy have a lady who is so understanding, who always puts me first and who loves me so much? I hope you know that I couldn't live without her and her love. She's my world, the thing that makes me tick.

I call Specs and he confirms that I can have three days, but no more. In the morning I'll catch the 9:30 Greyhound for Los Angeles.

# CHAPTER FORTY

THE RIDE ACROSS THE DESERT IS LONG, BUT I'M SO FILLED with anticipation of solving the case that I don't mind a single mile. The turning wheels are taking me closer and closer to the conclusion of a most frustrating story, as well as the chance to bring a killer to justice.

We pull into the big bus terminal and I make my way out to sun-drenched Main Street and into the hustle and bustle of the place they call "The City Of The Angels," the melting pot of the world. You can hear any language from any location on the globe. Down to my left, I see a giant billboard for the Orpheum Theater reading: "On Stage, Hal McIntyre and his Orchestra with vocalists Al Nobel and Ruth Gaylor."

I grab up a copy of the *Los Angeles Times* and step into a tiny open-air cafc just off the sidewalk. I enjoy a hot cup of coffee and a sweet roll. The *Times* has a wide selection of crime stories both solved and unsolved.

The national news includes the announcement that Benny Goodman, "The King of Swing," and the NBC Symphony Orchestra are going to premiere "Clarinet Concerto," by Aaron Copeland.

On the international scene the population of the world is now 2.3 billion, with the US population reading 150,697,999. Illiteracy is at 3.2 percent. I gulp down my breakfast, and trash the *Times* along with my paper cup and plate. Up the street I can see the large sign that marks the site of the Hotel Cecil.

I'm very tempted to make a quick stop at the Main Street Gym, to see what well-known fighters are working out, but I resist the urge and make straight for the hotel. With my suitcase in hand, I push through the revolving doors and make my way across the carpeted lobby. As soon as the desk clerk is free, I get his attention.

"I'm Gene McLain from the *Arizona Reporter*. I have a reservation for a single room. I called and made arrangements with the management to go through your old guest registers for possible clues to a double homicide."

"I was told you would be here this morning." He pushes the guest register toward me and I sign in. He gives me my room key. "Would you like to go to your room first, or would you like to be shown where the old guest registers are stored?"

I opt for finding the location of the registers. He offers to keep my suitcase behind the desk while the security officer on duty takes me to where I will be working. The clerk dials a number.

"Norm, Mr. McLain from the *Arizona Reporter* has arrived. He's here at the front desk. Could you take him down to where the ledgers are stored? Very good. I'll tell him. Mr. McLain, our security chief, Norman Jackson, will be here in just a second. He will take you to the storage area."

I thank him and stand off to the side of the desk, watching the ebb and flow of people as they cross and re-cross the carpeted lobby. I've always been a "people watcher" and this is an excellent vantage point from which to study the human condition. A rugged man in his early forties steps up and sticks out his right hand.

"Norman Jackson is the name. I'm head of security. The

office told me you would be with us a few days going through the old guest ledgers." He looks me up and down, then smiles. "I hope those are old clothes. It's pretty dusty and dirty downstairs."

"I'll change clothes before I start to work, but if you could show me how to find the materials I'm after, then I won't have to bother you again."

We move through the lobby to the bank of elevators, and get the first one available. Norm had told the truth. This place is really the pits. Way back into the corner of the dark and dank basement is a bin piled high with ledgers that are covered with spider webs and their occupants, as well as what seems to be a ton of rat droppings. There *is* dirt and dust everywhere. All this beauty is lit by a single 40 watt bulb hanging at the end of a long cord.

"Here you are. Those are all the old records and there's plenty of them."

To say I'm having a sinking feeling is putting it mildly. "How about that. There must be records dating back to the day this hotel opened." I pick up a couple of mildewed ledgers. Blowing the dirt, dust and rat droppings off the covers, I work my fingers through the spider webs and send a couple of mean looking creatures onto the floor.

Jackson gives me a quizzical look. "How long do you have to work on this project?"

"Exactly three and one-half days. At noon, Sunday, I have to be on the Greyhound for Phoenix. Right now, I want to get to my room, change my clothes, and get to work."

We ride up to the main floor where I retrieve my suitcase.

"Good luck, Mc Lain, and happy hunting. If there's anything I can do for you, give me a call."

"In fact, there is something you can do for me. What are the chances of getting a 100 or 150 watt bulb to replace the one in the storage bin?"

"When you come down, stop by the desk. I'll leave a 150 with the clerk."

We shake hands and I take the elevator up to the third floor where my room is located. The enormity of the task I have set for myself hits me like a rock dropped from the top of the Empire State Building.

# CHAPTER FORTY-ONE

DAYS RUN INTO NIGHTS AND NIGHTS INTO DAYS. I HAVE established a routine. A quick breakfast in the coffee shop where the waitress on duty has the chef sack up a sandwich and a Coke for my lunch, so I don't have to take a break. When the end of my day comes, it's long after midnight. I pray no one will be on the elevator to see a man who looks more like a coal miner coming up out of the pits after a day's work in the mines than a guest in the hotel.

One morning, a lady in an elegant gown demanded that the gentleman she was with get off at the next floor and wait for another elevator rather than to ride with the likes of me. I don't blame her. Stumbling into my room, I take a hot shower, fall into bed and before I know it, the desk is giving me the wake-up call and another grueling day begins.

I am very much aware that the seconds, minutes, and hours are slipping away. I find an empty crate that serves as my chair and I work in the center of the bin with the filthy ledgers piled on all sides. I've gotten used to the rats who run over my feet and love to scramble over the piles of books. The roaches look at me from the edge of the circle of light and the spiders are very angry with me for destroying their webs.

I've been here for three days. Now it's Sunday, and I have to check out and be at the station at twelve noon sharp when the bus pulls out for Phoenix. Unless I have mixed the ledgers up, I figure I have nine to go. The dirt streaked face of my wrist watch tells me it's 10:30 AM. I grab one of the remaining nine ledgers and as I have done with all the ledgers before, I work my finger slowly down each page reading name after name.

I stop. I stand, wipe my hand over my bleary eyes and make myself read aloud very, very slowly. *"Charlie Andrews, Arizona State College, Tempe, Arizona"*

Gotcha! How about that? I carefully tear the page bearing Charlie Andrews' name out of the ledger, turn off the light, and leave the basement to the spiders, roaches, and rats.

Back in my room, I sing during my shower. Though I haven't slept for the last twenty-four hours, I feel fresh and ready to go. A good shave adds to the feeling of well being. I throw my dirty clothes into the suitcase, and take the elevator to the lobby.

"How did it go Mr. McLain? Did you find the evidence you were looking for?"

"It couldn't have gone better. If you have my bill, I'll pay it and hustle down to the bus station. I don't want to miss my ride home."

I push through the doors of the hotel, stop, and take a few deep breaths of fresh air. A light drizzle is falling. I say something about the rain to the doorman, who acts as though I must have dropped in from Mars since it has been raining for two days. Hurrying down the street, I look across at the Main Street Gym and see they have a new poster on the wall by the entrance. Through the drizzle, I can make out the name "Sugar Ray" Robinson, but the rest is lost behind the falling rain and the endless traffic hurtling by. No doubt, Ray Robinson is the greatest fighter pound for pound in the entire world, but since I'm running so close to departure time, I don't dare cross the street to read the rest of the information.

The rain becomes heavier as I reach the Arizona state line. It's putting it down first class by the time I arrive in Phoenix. I grab my bag and rush through the swinging doors of the terminal. A honking horn alerts me to the fact that Blondie is pulling in behind the car that's pulling out. The kids scramble out for hugs and kisses, then I hurry them into the back seat and out of the rain, along with my suitcase.

I slide in by Blondie and, as always, I'm blown away by her beauty. She comes into my arms for a super kiss, then asks, "Well?"

"I got him. Now I know who the killer is. He's been right here under our noses all this time. His name is Charlie Andrews and he's a student at Arizona State."

"You did it!"

Blondie flies into my arms and we hug and kiss, to the delight of the children. Someone behind us leans on their horn, which brings us back to reality.

"Let's go home and get this gang to bed, sweetheart," I say. "Tomorrow, I'm going to get Charlie Andrews."

# CHAPTER FORTY-TWO

THE TELEPHONE IS RINGING AND BLONDIE PICKS IT UP.

"McLain residence. Yes, he's here. I'll get him."

At that moment, I enter the kitchen. Blondie holds the phone against her body and speaks in a whisper. "It's Specs. Something urgent."

I'm feeling like a million dollars ready to go nail Charlie Andrews, and now Specs is about to turn my world upside down. Well, after all, he is the boss, so here goes. I get a pad and pencil and take the phone from Blondie.

"McLain here. Where?"

I scribble the address on the notepad by the phone.

"Okay, I'm on my way."

I hang up and turn to my beautiful wife.

"A society woman has been murdered out in Paradise Valley. Specs got a tip on the killing and we can get the cover story if I get there fast enough."

"Go ahead, honey. I'll drop the kids off at school. If you're going to be late, call Mom. I know she'll be happy to pick them up and take them home with her. Did Specs inquire about the results of your trip to LA?"

"Not a word. He's written this off as the perfect crime, just like the police, and I'm not going to mention that I know who the killer is."

She stands on her toes and gives me a kiss. "Don't be upset about Specs. As for Charlie Andrews, he has no idea that you know who he is. Tomorrow or the next day, you'll wrap that up. Go ahead, honey. This may be a big story."

Larry and Jerry dash in, ready for school. Jerry announces, "Okay Dad, we're ready to go."

Larry is bouncing around like a rubber ball. "I get to sit up front today. Right Dad?"

I slip my .38 into the holster on my belt and pull my shirt over it. "I'm afraid you boys will have to work that out with your mother. Dad just got a priority call. I have to go."

I squat down and take a boy in each arm. "You guys know that Dad loves you more than anything in the whole wide world. You also know that Dad has to keep working, so we can have a nice home and clothes and all the things we enjoy. Be good guys and do what your mother tells you. With just a little bit of luck, maybe we can go on a picnic next Sunday." I kiss the boys and go out to my car.

# CHAPTER FORTY-THREE

THE DAYS OF RAIN HAVE MADE EVERYTHING FRESH AND GREEN. Since I'm on the road early, the traffic is light. I drive up to the swanky address that Specs gave me and find an unmarked police car parked in the secluded drive. I take my camera and walk to where Detectives Corrigan and Palumbo are standing. Corrigan is smoking a thin cigar and both men look anything but happy.

"Dare I say, top O' the mornin' to you two fine lads? You both looked as if the proverbial roof had caved in. What's the story?"

Palumbo jerks his thumb toward the entrance. "We have a top priority inside. It's so much a priority that Chief Bleiler has sent our beloved Chief of Detectives, 'Honest' Jack Dean, to supervise the handling of this case. Come on inside before the other news media show up."

Corrigan throws away what's left of his cigar and joins us as we move inside the luxurious mansion.

"This place is going to be crawling with reporters. This story is going to be a hot potato, otherwise Jack Dean would never be personally involved."

We walk through the fabulous dwelling that has to have

cost in excess of two million to build. We arrive at the master bathroom where a strikingly beautiful woman lies dead in a sunken bathtub. I get busy snapping a series of pictures to go with my story. The water still contains a blanket of tiny bubbles from her bubble bath. The water beneath the white froth is red. The woman appears to be in her early forties, but she is very well preserved. With makeup, I would think a lot of people would guess she would be in her early thirties.

I move around Palumbo, who's consulting his notepad.

"You're looking at Kathleen Johnson, age forty-two. She's 5'4", one hundred ten pounds, give or take a pound or two. She's the former Kathleen Burford. At one time, she was New York's most dazzling debutante. Her family has money they haven't counted and her marriage only added more big money to the coffers. Bob can tell you about her husband."

"Flagg—now isn't that a hell of a first name? F-L-A-G-G, better known as Sonny Johnson, is a big, and I mean big, player in international investments. He has pieces of all kinds of industry around the world and he is a major force in the stock and bond markets. He also has some major investments in a couple of Las Vegas casinos. He's a top flight polo player, and has been known to extend a couple of top professionals to the limit of their talents on the tennis court. The Johnson's have a home on the ocean in La Jolla, California, a penthouse in downtown Manhattan, an apartment in Paris, a townhouse in Bermuda and a ski chalet in Switzerland. I don't want you to think that you're dealing with poverty row."

Chief of Detectives, Jack Dean, enters. Six foot two, with a touch of grey at the temples. Jack should have been a lawyer. He would be one of the great ones. He has a razor-sharp mind, can deliver the finest speech you have ever heard, plus he's a likeable no-nonsense kind of guy. For him to be here means that the word from Chief Weldon Bleiler is to wrap this up ASAP.

"Hi, McLain. Looks as though you have a super scoop.

This one will be covered by major publications both here and abroad." He turns to Palumbo and Corrigan. "Doc Pearis and the boys are on the way. Stay on top of this and keep me updated. The Chief wants this solved as quickly as possible. If you need me, I'll be at my office. I'll see if the hotline stays open." Jack gives a general nod to all of us and is gone.

I'm trying to see through the bubbles surrounding the corpse.

"What was the cause of death?"

Corrigan looks down with that detached air he always has with a corpse. "She took three rounds from a .38 in her belly. All indications are that she started to stand up, but the slugs took her down. One went clear through her and into the water. I pulled it out and sacked it for ballistics."

"How long do you think she's been dead?"

Palumbo consults his notes. "According to the maid, who has been on vacation, she found the body when she reported for work this morning, around eight AM."

Corrigan is sitting by the edge of the tub watching the slight movement of the water around the still figure. "We got here about thirty minutes ago and the water in the tub was still luke-warm."

"Has anyone notified her husband?"

Corrigan stands and he has the same look in his eyes that he had when he was interrogating Jose Quintero down at headquarters. "I'd like to find him. There is no evidence of forced entry and, to date, he's my number one suspect."

With Mrs. Johnson being a member of international society, the AP wire and all the other news media will give this top priority status. I need to get my story together.

Palumbo snaps shut his notepad and gives me a reminder: "The fact that the Johnsons are *big* donors to a variety of Phoenix and world-wide charities, as well as being patrons of the arts, means that the screws will be on until this case is solved."

There are sounds of confusion as Doc Pearis and his crew move into the master suite. I hear the Doc's distinctive voice from down the hall. "OK, fellows—come on, let's give the old Doc a little room, so I can give you the low-down on this stiff."

I move away from the action and look for the maid. This story has to start somewhere. Since I was not on the scene when the person or persons unknown squeezed the trigger, I have to find a place to start the weave of words that will soon be hitting the local front page, as well as the AP wire. A young uniformed officer tells me to go through the library where I'll find the maid on the rear patio.

From the number of trophies displayed in the library, I would guess that Sonny Johnson spends more time on the golf course than he does in his office. In and around the trophies are lots of pictures of Sonny with various celebrities. It's not the celebrities that catch my eye. It's an eight by ten color photo taken at the Camelback Inn. There, big as life, is Sonny Johnson with his golf partner, Mr. Bill Broaddus of Acme Motors. I have a distinct feeling that Mr. Broaddus and I will be meeting soon.

The interview with the maid goes as well as expected. She loves her employer and has been with them for eight years. In fact, she had been employed by Mrs. Johnson while she lived in New York and moved west after the marriage. Outside of saying that once in a while Sonny drank a little too much, I gather, at least from her version, that this couple had a marriage made in heaven.

I ask her if she happens to know Mr. Broaddus. She tells me that he is one of Sonny's best friends. She also supplies Mr. Broaddus' home address, which dictates my next stop.

# CHAPTER FORTY-FOUR

BILL BROADDUS HAS A BREATH-TAKING LAYOUT. IT'S THE KIND of digs you see profiled in *Architectural Digest.* He has at least a million-dollar view of Squaw Peak. His estate is gated, but the gates are open, so I cruise in and take the big circular drive that brings me to the front of his palatial home. There's a spanking new white Jaguar convertible, black top down, with Montana plates sitting by the Spanish tile entryway that leads past a softly bubbling fountain near the tall double doors that lead into the house.

I'm happy to find that Mr. Broaddus is a subscriber to the *Reporter.* The morning edition is against the door. I pick it up and note that a tiny sidebar informs the citizens of the USA that President Harry Truman is sending military advisors to a place called the Republic of South Vietnam. I think I have a pretty good handle on world geography. However, I'd bet ninety-nine percent of Americans don't know anything about Vietnam or where it's located. I push the buzzer and deep chimes ring inside. A smiling young Mexican houseboy in a sparkling white jacket bids me welcome and directs me to the den, informing me that Mr. Broaddus will be with me in a couple of minutes.

If I thought Sonny Johnson's trophy room was something special, this den—with a wall of glass that gives you a dazzling view of the valley—is the ultimate. Golf and tennis trophies are everywhere and the three walls that are not glass have an amazing collection of photos.

The houseboy, who tells me his name is Manuel, pushes a rolling cart into the den. It features a beautiful silver urn that is filled with ice cold Bloody Mary's. I take him up on his offer and he serves me one in a tall glass etched with the Broaddus crest. When he leaves, I wander around looking at the photos. There are several of Bill and Sonny at various tournaments but the one that hangs by the fireplace is most revealing in more ways than one.

There, seated on a diving board is the lovely Rosemary Williams better known as Mrs. George Williams. Her voluptuous body covered only by small strips of cloth in strategic places leaves very little to the imagination. Those beautiful green eyes look straight into mine and the smile is dazzling. Most interesting is the inscription. "To Billy, the best lover and sweetest guy I have ever known." Hey, score one for our boy Billy Broaddus.

I hear his voice in the hall and seconds later he comes through the door decked out in tennis whites with a knockout brunette, who I would guess to be twenty-one or twenty-two, also in tennis attire. She's got a shape like a Vargas drawing and tanned legs that seem to go on forever.

"Mr. McLain, what a surprise. I see Manuel got you started with a morning eye-opener. By the way, say hello to Suzy Janis."

I say my hellos while Billy gets a couple of Bloody Marys assembled. It gives me time to find out that Suzy is from Montana. She's from a family that owns a lot of Montana's oil and a huge spread of cattle. She's spending a week at the Broaddus hacienda.

Bill tells me that he and Suzy have an early tennis date at

the country club. I ask him if we could have a couple of minutes in private. Suzy goes into a pout.

"You've had me up for hours. I'm hungry. I want to go to the club, now!"

"Honey, just give me a couple of minutes with Mr. McLain and we'll head for the club and have breakfast, plus some wonderful tennis."

With her drink in hand, she stomps out of the room. When the doors close behind her, Bill gives me a sheepish grin.

"These young ones have their appeal, but not in a long race. A couple of more days and I'll be happy to send her back to Big Sky Country and all that oil and cattle money. Now, what is it you want to talk to me about?"

I give him the news of Kathleen's murder and the fact that Sonny is missing. He's shocked. He says all the right things and hopes that her killer will be brought to justice. He assures me there is no way that Sonny would have killed his wife. Oh, they had their troubles, but no more than most married folks.

Sometimes you get razzle-dazzled so long by smooth operators that when you find a chink in their armor you can't resist giving them the needle and watching them squirm. I thank Billy for my drink then, with a choir boy's look of innocence on my kisser, I point to the photo of Rosemary Williams. "I had no idea that you're such a good friend of Mrs. Williams."

Billy sets his drink down hard on the edge of his desk and his face turns dark red. "We were never really good friends. She just got carried away when she signed that picture."

I have to hand it to Bill. He did a recovery that even the District Attorney would have been proud of. In my book, when you spend a lot of intimate time with a lady you are, like it or not, some kind of friends. As Harry Morse would say, there's no use beating a dead horse, but I have to give one more little jab as I make my exit. "Maybe that's true. However,

I would say she is a *very* good friend of a guy named Johnny Saita up in Las Vegas."

His eyes bug and his mouth opens and closes like a fish out of water, but nothing comes out. He's still standing in the den as I make my way out to my wheels.

Suzy is sitting on the driver's side of the Jag with those long legs draped over the door. She jerks upright.

"I hope you're satisfied—you've made me starve. Get that junk heap that passes for a car out of here."

I get my wheels, but I slow down as I pass her and give her a big smile and a wave. "Have a nice day."

She yells a few unprintable words at me as I depart. For some reason, I feel that this is not going to be a breakfast and morning of tennis to be remembered.

# CHAPTER FORTY-FIVE

NEXT STOP IS THE OFFICE OF JOHNSON INTERNATIONAL Investments, where all the workers have nothing but good to say about their boss and his wife. Although, they didn't see Mrs. Johnson often. They thought she was a beautiful and kind lady. I'm having a hard time trying to put together why anyone would harm the Johnsons. With no forced entry, this had to be an inside job, but who? In the meantime, a statewide dragnet is out to locate Sonny, but as of this hour the results are zero.

I talk with the bankers who take care of both the business and personal accounts for the Johnsons, and as far as what can be determined, there's nothing wrong in the financial picture of these beautiful people.

I phone in my cover story. It will be printed under the photo I have taken of the deceased in her final bubble bath. In the meantime, I have criss-crossed this valley and talked with everyone I can find who has anything to do with either Sonny or his socialite wife. This includes mechanics, society matrons and heads of charities that the Johnsons have endowed. Business men who have dealt with the Johnsons' company both in Arizona and in major cities around the world have nothing but the highest praise for Sonny as a business man and friend. If these people are so wonderful, why is one of them lying on a slab in the morgue with a belly full of lead?

It's the following morning, and the trail is as cold as it was yesterday—about as active as a deep freeze. Sonny Johnson has disappeared and some wags are betting that he's been kidnapped and will be found dead. That makes no sense at all. If Sonny is dead, who'd pay the ransom?

Specs calls me in to see if I have covered the case like a blanket. He's getting a lot of pressure from publisher David V. Sacks who's a close friend of the Johnsons. As Corrigan and Palumbo have predicted, the squeeze is on from the Governor to the Police Chief to wrap this up. I check my messages and find nothing of importance. I wander down to The Eagle, having called Blondie to see if she could make an early lunch.

Mary O. is all smiles when I come in and Jo Oakes can't give us service fast enough. I chuckle at how everything comes back to normal once McLain rights his world.

We talk about the Johnson case. Blondie tells me that it is bedlam over at headquarters. The phones are ringing constantly from various parts of the world with people wanting an update on this case. I point out to her that nothing like this happened regarding the missing persons case. I also remind her of my frustration in not being able to go after Charlie Andrews, as if she doesn't know. As always, Blondie is the calming influence. She encourages me to keep focused on the Johnson case and Charlie Andrews will keep.

I pay the bill, walk outside, and give Blondie a smooch. I watch that beautiful figure make its way across the street. She gives me a wave at the top of the courthouse steps, then she's gone.

# CHAPTER FORTY-SIX

I'VE SPENT TOO MANY YEARS ON THE STREET NOT TO KNOW that a furtive word, or a telephone call out of the blue, can change the complexion of any case, anytime, anywhere. I have no expectation that this will happen in this case, but fate is about to show me how wrong I can be.

I drive out to beautiful Turf Paradise Race Track to talk with the trainer of five race horses owned by Sonny Johnson. His trainer, one Pete Marshall, probably knows as much about race horses as anyone. He's pleasant, knowledgeable in his profession, and when I quiz him at length about his employer, he, like everyone else, gives Sonny the highest marks. We finish our talk and I walk out to the rail and watch a couple of thoroughbreds work out. Going back to where my car is parked, I have to go by the jockey's room. As I'm passing, I hear somebody say my name in broken English.

The man who called to me is a young Cuban who is having a lot of success at the major tracks this season and Turf Paradise is no exception. Once he determines that I am, in truth, Gene McLain the homicide reporter, he asks if he can walk with me.

On the way to the car, he tells me that everything with

Sonny Johnson is not as it seems. According to him, Sonny has eyes for the pretty Latin ladies who are the lovers or wives of several of the jockeys now riding at the track. He gives me an address of a young Cuban girl who he says can tell me a lot about Sonny if I can, in turn, provide her with a few dollars.

After he goes back to the clubhouse, I give the situation a lot of thought before driving out of the parking area toward the address he left with me.

The place where Yolanda Solcedo—the young girl he told me about—lives is a run-down apartment building next to a parking lot for a department store which is on the edge of Phoenix's south side. Located a block from the store, the lot has attractive rates and is managed by a personable young man who is a football standout at Phoenix High School. I park and make some small talk with him. Then I make my way to the old apartment house.

There are no names on most of the mail boxes but Solcedo is scrawled with crayon on one for Apartment Nine, located on the second floor. I walk up the dark stairs and aromas of foreign foods sweep over me. Arriving at number nine, I knock twice and hear someone moving about, then the door opens.

Yolanda could be a double for screen actress Rita Hayworth, with one exception: the purple mass of swollen flesh that seals her left eye shut. Her jockey friend had alerted her to the fact that I would be showing up, so my being here is not a surprise.

Her story is old but in so many cases true. She had come to Phoenix with a young jockey from Cuba who had a bad season on the circuit. She was preparing to go to California with him where he was going to try his luck on the tracks of the Golden State when she came into the vision of horse owner and millionaire Sonny Johnson. It seems Sonny was aflame with passion for the young woman and encouraged her to remain in Phoenix. She knew he was married, but he promised true love and that he would get rid of his wife. His one stipulation was that she get rid of her current lover before he came to her bed with gifts and eternal love.

Though attracted by the handsome Sonny, who is wealthy and apparently oozes sexual appeal, she had hesitated for a few days before making the break with her jockey. On informing him that she was remaining in Phoenix, the young man produced a knife and threatened to cut her heart out.

In the end, he never struck her, cut her, or harmed her in any way. Three days after arriving in California, he was involved in an auto accident while driving at high speed on scenic Route 1 and will be a paraplegic for life.

Sonny took his time in coming for the "love of his life." He picked her up in his new Cadillac and took her to a dump of a motel near Apache Junction. She had expected, at the very least, to be taken to one of the fancy resorts around Phoenix, but here she was in a shack where the plain wood floor had an ancient throw rug and the faucets in the bathroom were broken. It was apparent that Sonny had been drinking heavily. There was no prelude to love. Instead, he ripped the clothing from her well rounded body and threw her on the bed. He stripped and made his way into the bed. According to Yolanda, he was endowed with almost equine proportions, but all this did him no good. The years of heavy drinking had rendered him impotent.

Yolanda tried all the methods known to arouse him. After repeated attempts to consummate his lust for the young girl, he turned violent and beat her, breaking several ribs and punching her in the eye. He warned her that, if she told the police, she would never see Cuba again. He claimed he had "the police department in his pocket," and anyway, who would believe her word against his?

She managed to pull her torn clothes together and called the jockey who had put me in contact with her to come and get her. He took her to the emergency room at St. Joseph's

Hospital where they bandaged her ribs and gave her some pain medication. She knew the doctor on duty did not believe she had "fell down stairs," but there was nothing he could do other than to release her.

During her story, she mentions that after Sonny was unable to perform, he cursed her and told her that she was a whore, just like his wife who sleeps with every man who comes along. Yolanda just wants bus fare to Miami. She has an aunt who can get her back to Cuba and she wants to go home.

It happens that I have my paycheck in my pocket. I tell her to get her things together and I will take her to the bus station and buy her a one-way ticket to Miami. Her things all fit in a small bag. I cash my check at the bank and we walk over to the bus station. Our timing is excellent, as a bus heading east is due to leave in five minutes.

I purchase the ticket and give it to her. We walk out on the platform. We wait until all the passengers have entered the bus and I hand her the little parcel of clothes and press two twenty dollar bills in her hand and mumble something about her having expenses on the trip. She kisses my cheek and tears fill her beautiful brown eyes as the door of the bus closes behind her.

I'm going to be on short rations this week, but what the hell. I'm getting signs of a spare tire that I don't need, so I can cut the food intake. I just hope that she never meets another Sonny Johnson and that her life in Cuba or wherever she stops proves to be a happy one.

# CHAPTER FORTY-SEVEN

I FIX DINNER FOR THE KIDS AND MYSELF AS BLONDIE IS working late. They agree that I'm not in their mother's league as a cook but they enjoy the pancakes and eggs, which are almost exclusively Sunday breakfasts. For them, it's a real treat.

After we eat and the dishes are washed, I call Palumbo at home. His lovely wife, Sandy, takes the call and gets Joe on the horn. I fill him in on the Yolanda-Sonny Johnson affair. He agrees that we better start looking under some other rocks. We might come up with a motive. He said that Corrigan is furious because the dragnet has failed to locate Sonny. Bob is one hundred percent certain that Sonny is the killer and wants him in the worst way.

Later, I tell Blondie Yolanda's story. She listens very patiently, although, I notice she squints her pretty eyes just a little bit when I tell her the part about buying the bus ticket and donating forty dollars to the "cause." Afterwards, she hugs me and tells me I'm just a sentimental Irishman. All that street talk about how tough I am has to be misinformation. She tells me she loves me and wouldn't trade me for anyone. That makes me feel pretty good—to know that my option is not up and I'm staying around. However, she does tease me about giving away my lunch money.

As she takes off the makeup and gets ready for bed, she tells me about her hectic day. Somewhere along the line, I drift off to dreamland thinking of all the guys who never tell their wives anything, but then, they don't have Blondie.

# CHAPTER FORTY-EIGHT

As usual, the *Reporter* is a version of bedlam this morning. Reporters writing stories, looking at photos, reading out-of-town newspapers and doing clip and paste. Copy boys are running and telephones ring non-stop.

I call Grasser at home and paint a word picture of the ugly side of Sonny Johnson. The cops have no leads and tomorrow we're into day four and nothing has moved forward.

I have high hopes that something will break on the Johnson case this morning. I want to go after Charlie Andrews, but I know that break or no break, I'm going to have to postpone reaching my target. The reason I knew this absolutely is because of the square envelope laying on my desk. It has a note clipped to it from Specs telling me to follow through.

In the state of Arizona, they send out engraved invitations to those who are invited to witness an execution. It is all very formal, and as I open it I realize that only the name of the condemned changes with each invite. This one reads: "Mr. Gene McLain, *Arizona Reporter,* The honorable Governor of the State of Arizona invites you to witness the execution of

Robert A. Kellogg next Wednesday, 10:00 PM at the Arizona State Prison, Florence, Arizona.

I don't think I've given Bob Kellogg a thought since the day the jury sentenced him to die in the gas chamber after just thirty minutes of deliberation. Since Kellogg had pleaded guilty, walking through the trial was just a formality. His public defender wanted to go for an insanity plea but the doctors who examined Kellogg found him as sane as the rest of us who are out on the street.

The murder happened on a train that was traveling through northern Arizona on the way to California. Kellogg, who has a rap sheet that covers all the bases except indecent exposure, was coming to the west coast to get away from the heat the cops in Chicago were making part of his daily life. During the long train ride, he noticed a widow who was wearing expensive jewels and carried a thick roll of bills. Kellogg struck up an acquaintance and, a couple of nights after sharing dinner, they had drinks in the club car.

Somewhere along the way, he made his play and the widow turned him down. Knowing that the following day the trip would be over, he managed to put the sharp steak knife he had used on his T-Bone at dinner into his jacket pocket.

At the trial, he gave a cock-and-bull story about self-defense. He claimed the widow had asked him to visit her in her compartment and had attacked him with a steak knife when he failed to succumb to her charms. There were plenty of witnesses who said it was plain the woman had washed her hands of him and his attempts to start an affair.

Since most of the passengers were asleep, and the few who were up were playing cards or drinking in the club car, it is assumed that he pretended to be the porter, and when she opened the door he forced his way in. When her body was discovered the next morning, her gown had been ripped off. She had been raped, then stabbed to death with a sharp steak knife. Her bankroll and jewels were gone. So was Robert Kellogg.

He had jumped from the train after the murder. For three or four days he eluded the posse and their dogs who hunted him down near the northern rim of the Grand Canyon. When they ran him to ground, he was mighty hungry after a long time without food. The blood stains on his clothes matched those of the widow and he had a hefty bankroll in his pocket. The jewels were never found and for all we know they may be somewhere in the bottom of the canyon or maybe hidden in a culvert where someone will discover them a hundred years from today. Mr. Kellogg is not telling where they are.

Since he dies tomorrow, Specs wants a feature for the morning edition, then coverage of the execution on Wednesday. Let's face it, McLain, there is no rest for the wicked.

I check in with Jack Dean to see what is new with the Johnson case. Palumbo had told him the story Yolanda Solcedo passed on to me and they're busy trying to find other leads, but to date, zero. I told Jack I had to go down to Florence to see everyone's favorite traveler, Robert Kellogg, and that if anything broke on the Johnson affair, to call me at the warden's office. Jack agreed, so I get my wheels and roll south.

It's hot and dusty and I don't feel much like sharing bon motts with Mr. Kellogg. I have to do my best to come up with a story that the readers will devour, although they should have taken Mr. Kellogg from the jail in Flagstaff and hanged him, saving themselves and the taxpayers a lot of money.

Kellogg is in prison denims. He will not get his "going away" outfit until tomorrow. He has gained weight since I saw him at the trial. He had been slender and carried his 6' 2" frame very well. He is not a good looking guy by any stretch of the imagination, but I can see where, when he was dressed up, he might have had some success with a series of not-too-bright ladies. When he was arrested, he was very sun-tanned and wind-burned. Now, his skin is sallow. His hair, which had been coal black at the trial, has some grey in it. He bemoans the fact that prison food has caused him to put on excess weight and that the lack of exercise has done something to his system to make his hair start turning grey.

I remind him that he doesn't have to worry about having a head of grey hair since that won't happen overnight and he hasn't put on so much weight he won't fit in the cold metal seat that has his name on it in the gas chamber. I can tell he doesn't appreciate my sense of humor. The feelings are mutual. I don't care much for him either.

We go back over the case and he dances through the whole bit about having to kill the woman in self-defense. Of course, he has no answers as to why he raped her or why he fled with her jewels and money. He claims to know nothing about her jewels, so that secret is going to the grave with him. The stolen bankroll, of course, was his, but he never got to spend a dime. I can't help but think what a bore this interview is. I could have written a piece from the files that would have had as much impact. Then all at once he gets my attention.

For the first time, he tells me he is anxious to die. I ask him why he has this desire. He tells me that at night, when it is silent on death row, he can hear the far away whistle of a train and it's driving him crazy. Even if he's sound asleep, he awakens when the whistle sounds and for an instant he thinks he's back in the compartment fighting the widow who is covered with blood. He's happy that this will be the last evening he will ever have to hear the whistle again. Otherwise, it's going to drive him crazy and, of course, he doesn't want to go crazy. They might overturn his verdict and take him to the state insane asylum. There he would be forced to hear the whistle for the rest of his life.

All the way back to Phoenix, I play with the way I'll write Kellogg's story. Then it hits me. Play up the whistle angle. The murdered woman's voice coming out of nowhere to accuse and haunt her killer. I go to my typewriter and knock out the feature without a single change. I drop it by Specs' office and leave it with his secretary.

Before departing, I check with Jack Dean. The answer is no progress. I head home to a household that sometimes seems like the only normal place in the whole universe.

# CHAPTER FORTY-NINE

ANOTHER DAY, ANOTHER PERIOD OF ENDLESS TIME, AND Charlie Andrews is still sitting in his classrooms not knowing that I'm about to spring the trap that will capture him. Tommy, my favorite copy boy, stops by my desk.

"Anything new on the rich woman's murder?"

"Not a word, Souper. We're now into the fifth frustrating day and there's nothing going on. The key is the husband but no one has been able to find him."

Someone on the floor yells for Tommy, and he takes off at a dead run.

My phone jangles. Joe Palumbo tells me they just found Sonny Johnson and I can ride with him. I tell him I'll meet him downstairs in three minutes. I grab my camera off the end of thc desk and set off at a run to Specs' office. He's just coming out the door, so the timing is perfect. "They found Sonny Johnson. I'm going to ride out with the police, so hold some front page space." For a change Specs looks happy.

"Great—get some pictures and weave a lot of background into your feature. This one will pull a lot of readers both here and on the AP wire."

I remind him that if I hurry, we have an exclusive.

"You've got it."

I start to hot-foot it for the door when I remember the invitation on my desk. "Specs, tonight is the Kellogg execution. It will be a page five or six story and the Warden will have to scramble to get enough witnesses for the front row of chairs. Nobody cares about this guy. How about letting Pam go cover this? The invitation is on my desk and if she calls the prison and tells them she's subbing for me, there will be no problem."

Specs doesn't like it, but he wants me on the Johnson story, so he says he'll call Pam and give her the assignment.

Pam Rushman graduated in journalism at the University of Michigan, and has been with the paper for a little better than four years. She's blonde and perky with a sparkling personality.

In my book, she has a lot of promise as an investigative reporter, but to date, Specs has had her covering society news and entertainment. She's asked me a couple of times if I could put in a word for her to get a shot at a feature. Well, I just put in the word. I have visions of her getting a little green when they give Kellogg the gas, but that's all a part of learning.

Palumbo and Corrigan pull up to the curb as I hit the street. I'm in the back seat in a flash and we're off and running. We hit the highway toward Sedona, and after a few miles into the pretty country that comes with the foothills, we pull off and park beside Dr. Pearis' station wagon and a black-and-white. Two officers in uniform are stationed in front of wood horses set up to block off a winding two-lane road that leads up the mountain. They let us through, and we hike up the canyon about sixty yards. There, right around the bend is a new black Cadillac sedan parked at a crazy angle. The door on the driver's side is open and a pair of legs encased in expensive slacks protrude. The unflappable Doc Pearis is standing by the Caddy as I walk up camera in hand.

"Get your pictures, McLain. The meat wagon is on the way and you can bet a slew of reporters from all the various media will be following. In fact, it won't be long until the reporters are thicker than flies."

I get to work snapping pictures from a variety of angles. "What do you make of it, Doc?"

"For my money, it's open and shut. A forest ranger found the body at dawn this morning and called in. Our pal, Sonny Johnson, now known as the corpse, left a letter. It's been dusted and bagged." He hands the letter to Joe then continues, "It's an old story and certainly not exclusive to the Johnson family. It seems the little woman was thirty years younger, and at seventy, Sonny wasn't cutting the mustard. In fact, he had been impotent for some time. I gather that in his prime, Sonny was considered a five-star stud and not being able to function drove him to consume more booze than he could handle. Then, he found out that his wife was having an affair with a young man who works in his company. The other morning, while she was having a relaxing bath, he walked in and bang, bang, bang. Three slugs from his .38 put an end to her story. He killed himself with a single shot to the head. I'm willing to bet you a million dollars that the .38 laying on the car floor is the same weapon he used on his wife."

There's nothing more to be gained here, so I'm more than ready to leave when Palumbo suggests "Let's get out of here."

Joe takes Sonny's letter from his inside pocket and hands it to me. "You can scribble what you want on the way back to Phoenix. It's Sonny's last words and the whole dirty story is there."

Corrigan joins us as we move down the trail at a trot. "By now all the news services have been alerted and I don't intend to spend the rest of the day answering the same stupid questions over and over again."

"If you boys will drop me by the paper. I'll turn in my

story and the negatives, and if Specs doesn't want a follow up, I'm going to get back to work on the missing persons case."

I should know by now that when I make a statement like that, I've just put a voodoo curse on the remainder of the day.

# CHAPTER FIFTY

SPECS WANTS A FOLLOW-UP FEATURE THAT TELLS THE WHOLE story on the Johnsons, including his wife's rise in the international social set and, of course, Sonny's spectacular career in the world of high-finance, plus all his athletic accomplishments. Add to that the pictures of Mrs. Johnson as a debutante, pictures of their society wedding (eight hundred guests for a sit-down dinner), their honeymoon, pictures with a galaxy of celebrities around the world, and to wind things up, pictures of the murdered Mrs. Johnson in her final bubble bath and Sonny's fadeout in his shiny Cadillac.

Specs has decided that, though he will let Pam cover the execution, he wants me to go along and, as he puts it, "show her the ropes."

Pam is more than a little nervous, yet anxious to do well on this, her first feature assignment. I don't bother to explain that this is a nothing execution. Kellogg is a stupid, vicious killer who has no "hook" to build even a good local story around—let alone national. Why should I rain on her parade? She's on an emotional high. In her mind, she equates this affair as equal to the execution of Bruno Richard Hauptman or Eva Coo.

I talk her into stopping for dinner at a little cafe in Florence Junction, but while I polish off a steak, potatoes, squash, coffee, and a piece of apple pie for dessert, she picks at a small green salad.

We get to the prison. While waiting for the walk to the death house, a couple of the old timers give me the buzz about bringing the good looking chick around and want to know if Blondie has been informed.

As I predicted, only a few witnesses show up, and most of these are police officers from the northern part of the state who had been involved in the hunt with the posse.

I notice Pam has beads of sweat on her forehead, and she looks a little pale. They usher Kellogg in. He's asked if he has anything to say and he states that he hopes they will hurry so he won't have to hear the whistle of the evening train.

He gets his wish. They strap him in fast. The chaplain says a few words and is out of there. The door is locked. When the warden pulls the switch that starts Mr. Kellogg to the here-after, Pam grabs my forearm with a grip of steel. She breathes heavily and her face glistens with sweat, although the room is very comfortable. I don't believe her eyes could open any wider without popping out.

In a couple of minutes, the doctor pronounces Kellogg dead and we file out. I've got to hand it to the girl. She hangs in there all the way, but as we walk across the prison yard, the sickness becomes too much and she has to heave. The other witnesses pass without a second look. They have seen a lot of people, including tough guys, get ill at executions. I give her my clean white handkerchief. In a little while, she says we can move on.

During the drive back to Phoenix, there is no conversation. I sing along with the radio. I drive her to the front of the *Reporter*. She assures me that she's okay. She says she has a headache, but she'll write her story, then go home and get some rest.

I still feel she's going to be a damn good reporter. Though there's not much to say about the Kellogg case, I have a gut feeling that it will be well-written and she'll get as much out of it as is possible. As for me, I'm going to get some sleep so I'll be ready to hunt down Charlie Andrews come tomorrow.

# CHAPTER FIFTY-ONE

IN THE NOT TOO DISTANT FUTURE, ARIZONA STATE COLLEGE IS going to reach university status. I can't believe the way it's growing. I know people think I've had too much sun when I predict that Arizona State will be on the same level as UCLA and the University of Southern California. In fact, not only will they have the same academic standards, but ASU will compete on the same level in athletics. Just mark that in your book and see if McLain's predictions come true.

Blondie has been loaned to the sheriff's department for a special investigation and she beat me out of the house this morning. I drop the kids off at school. Now, I'm wandering around the fringe of this fast growing institution of learning, trying to find Charlie Andrews' apartment. At last, I find the place, just off campus, and there's Charlie's name, as big as life, on the mailbox in the downstairs hall. I climb the stairs to the second floor. Someone's record player or radio is playing Nat "King" Cole's super hit, "Mona Lisa." The Cole voice and his keyboard work are pure magic.

Charlie's domicile is Apartment Seven. I knock and the door opens to reveal a striking young lady with fair skin and strawberry blonde hair. Now I know what I missed by not going to college.

"I'm Gene McLain of the *Arizona Reporter* and I'm looking for Charlie Andrews."

The stunning blonde gives me a Colgate toothpaste smile.

"Jean Deaton's my name. I'm Charlie's girlfriend. We're going to the movies this afternoon to see Edmund O'Brien in 'D.O.A.' Charlie's been wanting to see it and it closes today. He'll be back in just a couple of minutes. Won't you come in?"

Miss Deaton has kind of a breathless way of speaking that fits her personality. Since she gave me the invite, I enter the long sought after abode of Charlie Andrews. The apartment is cheerful, bright and sunny. I would guess this kind of setting is what one will find all over this vast nation of ours. It doesn't matter if the college is east, west, north, or south. There are pennants, photos, and posters at various places on the wall. There are two desks and two beds. Both beds are made, but one desk is covered with notebook paper, text books, and other assorted tools of higher learning. The clean desk has a calendar and a radio. Outside of the cluttered desk, the whole place is very neat and comfortable.

"Please, sit down, Mr. McLain."

I find a place on the chintz covered couch that sits between the two desks. Jean Deaton stands holding onto the back of the chair facing the cluttered desk.

"Jean—May I call you Jean?"

"Of course, Mr. McLain."

"Jean, have you known Charlie for long?"

The question evokes a silvery laugh and another Colgate smile. "Ever since our freshman year. Charlie and I met at the Ice Breaker Hop and we've been going steady ever since."

We both hear the sound of running feet pounding up the stairs. I move my right hand under my shirt, close to my .38, just in case. The door swings open and, unless I miss my guess, I'm face-to-face with Charlie Andrews. Yep, Charlie Andrews.

Five foot eight, sandy hair, blue eyes and a freckled face. Everyone's choice for the All-American college boy. To say I am in deep shock is to only touch the tip of the iceberg. I can't stop the words that come out of my mouth.

"*You're* Charlie Andrews?"

A big smile lights up the freckled face. "One and the same, and you're Gene McLain, the reporter. I've seen your picture in the paper. I want you to know I read all your stories. Jean and I are journalism majors and while she's looking at a career writing women's novels, after graduation I hope to land a job with a newspaper."

I hear what he's saying, but I'm still in shock over his appearance.

"Thanks for the compliment, Charlie." My mind is whirling and from somewhere I grab a straw before I sink completely.

"By the way, have you ever visited Los Angeles and stayed at the Hotel Cecil on Main Street?"

"Why?"

"Oh, I just wondered."

"As a matter of fact I did stay one night at the Hotel Cecil. It must have been two years ago. Sure—it was my sophomore year. A friend had tickets to the Rams-San Francisco 49'ers game. Something came up and he couldn't make it, so I took the tickets and stayed at the Hotel Cecil overnight. Why, is this important?"

"No, no. Somewhere I got my wires crossed and your name came up, but it's obviously a mistake. I'm looking for a tall, good looking college boy who has dark curly hair. This guy probably has a lot of girls chasing him and, oh yes, he just happens to be left handed."

Both Charlie and Jean laugh, and Charlie explains. "Sorry about the laughter, but you're not so far off. It sounds like you're talking about my roommate, Bobby Mason."

Charlie walks over to the corner where a large cork

bulletin board is hung and points to an enlarged photo in the upper left hand corner. "That's Bobby with the cute blonde."

I stand up and move to where he has pointed. The picture shows a handsome, sun-tanned young man in an Arizona State T-shirt and white shorts. His arm is around a beautiful young blonde who is dressed in a white tennis outfit. Bobby has a tennis racquet swinging from his left hand.

"Is Bobby a pretty good tennis player?"

"The best. The athletic department has been after him ever since he was a freshman to play varsity football, but Bobby won't budge. He turned down a lot of football scholarships so he could concentrate on his law studies."

Jean gets into the act. "He does a lot of concentrating on all the good looking girls."

"Tell me, Charlie, what time will Bobby be through with his classes today? I'd like to spend a couple of minutes with him."

"You won't be able to see him today. Bobby's up in Seattle. His father used to be a famous prosecuting attorney. Now he's in private practice. Bobby got a telegram that his father is very ill and he went home. In fact, the telegram is stuck in the corner of the desk calendar. The clean desk."

"I hope Bobby comes back soon," Jean says. "He's quite a ladies man and all the cute girls come around all the time looking for him. I want to keep Charlie straight."

Jean's statement gets a chuckle from Charlie, who gives her a squeeze as he looks at her with loving eyes.

"Charlie, do you have any objections if I look at the telegram?"

"No sweat. Bobby won't be back until his father is well, I'm certain of that."

Charlie is moving from one foot to the other and Jean is looking as though she would like to be off and running. "I don't mean to be rude, Mr. McLain, but Jean and I have to go now or we're going to be late for the movie—the last showing is today. Stay as long as you like. Just lock the door when you leave. I'm sorry you missed Bobby. I know he'd like to meet you. Maybe, if it's not too much trouble, I can come down to the *Reporter* someday and you can show me around?"

"Anytime, Charlie. Just give me a ring ahead of time so I'll be sure to be around. Nice meeting you, Miss Deaton. I hope to see both of you again."

# CHAPTER FIFTY-TWO

THEIR FEET RACE DOWN THE STAIRS AND I HEAR THE DOOR close behind them. It's very quiet now. All the students must be somewhere else at this time of day. I walk over to where the photo of Bobby Mason and the blonde is mounted and I pull the thumb tacks. Young Mr. Mason is truly handsome. I can see how he's a lady killer. It's the other kind of killer I'm worried about. The smile in the photo is charming, but it seems like there is something hidden behind the eyes. The eyes give me an almost sinister feeling. I stroll over to the clean desk that belongs to Bobby, pick up the telegram, and read it.

"Bobby (stop) Come home at once (stop) Your father is very ill (stop) Advise as to what time you will arrive (stop) Love, Mother."

The telegram was sent the day before Williams, Severson, the client and car vanished. Can it be that this is a blind lead? Maybe Bobby Mason is not the man I'm looking for? Under the telegram is a business card. I pick it up and read, "Robert P. Mason, Sr., Attorney At Law, Seattle, Washington."

I put the card back where I found it and open the door to the hall when a bell goes off in the back of my mind. I close the door and return to Bobby's desk, pull out his chair, and sit down. Don't ask me why, I don't know. Call it intuition, call it luck, call it whatever you want, but something inside tells me that I am on the brink of finding the key to the puzzle. It is within my reach. I lean back in the chair and open the center drawer of the desk. There, neatly bound, lies a thesis. The title, in bold print, jumps out at me as I read, *Components Of Murder.*

"These five components are requisite to obtain conviction for murder." A list follows the masthead.

Number one. The Corpus or Body
Number two. The Opportunity for Murder
Number three. The Absence of Alibi
Number four. The Motive
Number five. The Detection and Arrest of the
Criminal.

Three spaces down is the word *Note* in italics. *"If a person is able to eliminate Item Three, The Absence of Alibi and Item Four, The Motive, they will wipe out Number Five, The Detection and Arrest of the Criminal. If that is done, you have a Perfect Crime."*

I read and re-read the front page of the thesis. For a long time, I'm lost in thought about what my next step in this investigation can mean to me, the paper, the killer, the survivors and a lot of other people whose lives are about to be changed forever.

At last, I pick up the business card and dial the number of Robert Mason, Sr., Attorney At Law, Seattle, Washington. After two rings, a secretary answers the phone identifying Mason's law office. "This is Gene McLain, of the *Arizona Reporter* newspaper in Phoenix, Arizona. I'm aware that Mr. Mason is ill, but it is very important that I make contact with his wife or some member of his family. Could you give me his home number?"

The secretary informs me that I am wrong. According to

her, Mr. Mason has never been sick a day in his life and is in the office as we speak. I ask her if I can speak with Mr. Mason. In a few seconds, a deep, resonant voice announces that I am speaking with Robert P. Mason, Sr.

"Mr. Mason, I'm Gene McLain, of the *Arizona Reporter* newspaper in Phoenix, Arizona. I'm calling about your son Bobby. I know that he attends law school at Arizona State, but I wonder if by any chance he might happen to be in your office now."

Mason informs me that his son has not been home since the start of the year and I must be mistaken about his being in Seattle.

"Mr. Mason, I have here in my hand a telegram supposedly sent by your wife asking Bobby to come home because you were ill."

Mr. Mason tells me that the telegram is some kind of hoax, some college prank. He has never been sick and Bobby is not home, but in school. As an afterthought, he asks if Bobby is in some kind of trouble.

How do you tell a parent that their world is crashing down on them ... that the child they love with all their heart and soul has crossed a line from which he can never return? That from this second on, this family will have grief and sorrow that will be with them 'til the end of their days? I suppose Billy Graham or Bishop Fulton Sheen or a lot of other people could find a better way to say it. I only know my way.

"Mr. Mason, your son is in the worst kind of trouble— your son is a murderer."

I hang up the phone with sympathy for this father flooding my soul. I look down at the thesis, take a black pencil from my pocket and check off Item One, The Corpus or Body and Number Two, The opportunity for murder. This is Bobby's road map and if I can follow it, the end will come in the gas chamber.

# CHAPTER FIFTY-THREE

THE START OF A BEAUTIFUL SUNSET IS PAINTING THE SKY AS I park in front of J.W. "Benny" Benjamin's Desert Used Cars. Benny is giving his Class-A sales pitch to a young couple looking at a station wagon. I must say that "Benny" really works at his profession. I watch him give the young people his business card as they walk off the lot. Benny is wiping the sweat from his face as he walks over to his office.

"I didn't get 'em on the dotted line, but I'll bet you they come back. That's a sweet little wagon for the price and the young lady is pregnant, and that will swing the deal. What's up, McLain?"

I flash the picture I took from Charlie Andrews' wall. I've cut the blonde out of the photo so only Bobby Mason remains.

"That's the kid. No doubt about it. This is the kid who bought the old Ford and paid cash."

A half-hour later I re-play the same scene with Bill Broaddus at the Acme Auto Agency. "That's him! That's the guy who took a ride with Williams and Severson in my apple red convertible."

I stop by O'Neill's office at the courthouse, but the coun-

164

selor left at noon for a game of golf and won't be back until morning. I tell his secretary that I have a hot lead on the missing person's case. She looks at me like O'Neill has already told her I was "a little out of touch."

You know how you can go to an office for a job interview and the person you are supposed to see is not in, but from the people there you get the feeling that you can come back one hundred times and you'll never get the job? That's exactly the way things strike me at O'Neill's office.

I'm not a guy that likes a lot of red tape or waiting or fooling around trying to get someone to move on something I know is the truth. So, I go to the place where I always go when I'm up against the wall, back to my typewriter at the *Reporter*.

I go down to the composing room just as Ben and his helpers are putting the finishing touches on tomorrow's paper. I haven't seen Ben since the discovery of the bodies and he is delighted to see me as I race in with a copy and a photo in hand.

"Well young fella', you sure made those fancy Dans eat their words. No one was as surprised as old Specs when you found those missing men."

"You're right on target, Ben. Specs was overjoyed."

"I'm so happy that you have been vindicated. What's this copy and photo you have for me?"

"This is front page as well as a syndicated special for the AP wire. I want to be certain this story is national news tomorrow morning."

"Just count on me, Gene.

"Front page for the *Reporter* and top priority for AP. I've got all the bases covered."

Tonight is one of those nights that the Chamber of Commerce writes about. The breeze is just right and the black velvet sky is filled with stars that shine like diamonds. I'm always amazed that in the southwest it seems the stars are so much closer than anywhere else in the world. During my hitch in the Navy, I would tell my shipmates that you could almost touch the stars when you were in Arizona. I don't know if they believed me, but it's true. You can't help but feel good when Mother Nature gives you such a sparkling display and the price is right.

For a change, both Blondie and I are home at a decent hour. So, we pack the kids in the car and take them to the pizza parlor where we can all stuff our faces and the kids howl at the old silent "Our Gang Comedy" movies they're showing. We finish eating, but have to stick around for two more showings. The kids love it.

Back home Blondie gets the little ones ready for bed and I get the percolator fired up and the coffee brewing. The kids show up for their goodnight kiss and Blondie and I get them settled in bed, then go back to the living room and relax. I can tell that Blondie is chomping at the bit to know what I had found out at Arizona State. She no sooner sits down than she is off and running.

"Did you get any leads regarding Charlie Andrews?"

"Honey, Charlie Andrews is not the target. His name was used by a college roommate, a young student named Bobby Mason, who happened to remember that Charlie had stayed at the Hotel Cecil in Los Angeles when he went over to see a pro football game. Mason's father is a big time attorney in Seattle."

"So, you're going to interview Mason and then make your case with the D.A."

"Wrong. Forget the interview. First of all, Bobby Mason is not around and, even if he was around, we wouldn't be doing an interview, at least not until after he's arrested. Bobby Mason is a killer and he's armed and dangerous. I stopped by O'Neill's office to fill him in, but he was playing golf. I left word with his secretary that I had a hot lead in the case and she was so disinterested that I'm not certain she heard what I said."

"Tomorrow morning you better get a hold of Chief Bleiler and the DA, so they can start the manhunt."

"Forget waiting on the Chief and the DA. Tomorrow morning the entire USA will know this killer is on the loose."

Blondie spills her coffee as she comes out of her easy chair like she was fired from a cannon.

"You've done it! Are you crazy? Tell me, have you done the same thing you did when you broke the story and the pictures of the murdered men?"

"Yes, and I was right."

"Oh, my God. I can't believe this. Did it ever enter your mind that you might not be as lucky this time? That boy's parents will sue the paper, and you. On top of everything, you'll be fired and then we'll lose everything we have worked so hard to get. How could you do this after what we went through before?"

I'm up on my feet and pacing. I know what Blondie says is true, but I also know that first, last and always, I'm a homicide reporter.

"Blondie, believe me. I'm right. I know I'm right and as I told you before, nothing is going to happen to us or the kids."

I'd give a million dollars if I could wipe that look of pain and fear off of my wife's beautiful face.

"Gene, how can you be so sure?"

With that, she collapses into her chair, and a trickle of tears rolls down her cheeks. I sit on the arm of the chair and take her hands in mine. She looks up at me with those lovely eyes all wet and misty and says. "Tell me, what is the world going to read tomorrow?"

# CHAPTER FIFTY-FOUR

A COPY OF THE FRONT PAGE OF THE *REPORTER* IS SPREAD OUT over Specs' desk. The big black headlines read, "**WHERE IS THIS KILLER?**" Underneath is the face of smiling, handsome Bobby Mason.

Just as I'm admiring the layout, a cane slashes down across the copy and the sound that follows is like the firing of a high-powered rifle. The cane belongs to David V. Sacks, owner and publisher of the *Reporter*. Specs' office is packed to the brim with startled spectators including the DA, old Ben, Specs, his secretary Jan, Joseph, Sacks chauffeur and, of course, yours truly. The decibel level is at the max as Sacks speaks.

"McLain, your career was saved by a fluke. When that Mexican found those bodies it was the luckiest day of your life. But you couldn't leave well enough alone, could you? You had to plaster this all over the country. You're calling this young man a killer. Don't you know that the law says you're innocent until proven guilty?"

The DA pulls himself up to his full height and enters the act at his pompous best. "That's what I've always tried to tell him ..."

Sacks comes unglued. "Shut up, O'Neill. You do your

talking at the courthouse. I'm talking now. McLain, don't you have brains enough to know this man is the son of a famous attorney? He'll sue me and this paper for every nickel we'll make for the next hundred years."

I didn't think it possible, but he turns the decibel level up another notch.

"Do you hear me, McLain? You and your stupid story have ruined my financial empire and I'm not going to let you get away with it."

I'm really tired of his raving. While he takes a deep breath to mount another assault, I take center stage.

"What's ruined is Bobby Mason's life, the lives of his parents, the men he murdered, and the people who survive them. As far as his father suing the paper, forget it. He's going to be too busy trying to keep his kid out of the gas chamber."

Sacks' eyes get narrower during my little speech and he pounces like a cat catching a mouse.

"You have no proof that this boy killed anyone."

"I've been a homicide reporter since I was eighteen years old. I've seen 'em all. Bobby Mason is a killer and I know how he thinks. He has an inflated ego and I'm willing to bet he still has the murder weapon in his possession. This guy thinks he's pulled off a perfect crime. He spent hours thinking about it. He wrote about it. Right here, I have his thesis. '*The Five Components Of Murder.*' It's a map of his twisted desires. I've checked off all but two of the five points. The ones remaining are 'The Motive' and 'The Detection and Arrest of the Criminal." I'll hound him until he's arrested and then I'll come up with the motive. I'm going to nail him. I'll show him the same mercy he showed those two car salesmen and I'll be there writing the story when he's strapped in the gas chamber."

You can hear a pin drop. Not even a foot shuffles. Sacks gets a cunning look on his face. The rage is under control now and I can tell his mind is racing a mile a minute with some devious scheme. When he speaks, it's with a well-modulated voice.

"A few 'Story Of The Year' awards seemed to have clouded your judgment, McLain. You've become judge, jury, and executioner. On the other hand, I'm a very compassionate man who is well aware that you have a lovely wife and two small children. I have the power to end your career as a reporter with a snap of my fingers and if I do, every newspaper publisher will applaud my actions. However, being the generous man that I am, I'm going to make you a proposition that I don't think you can refuse. You've put this paper in jeopardy with your story about the missing men. I was kind enough to give you forty-eight hours to find the bodies. Being very, very lucky, you were able to do that. This time, though, you're beyond the limit. Today's Thursday, the clock tells me it's 2:00 PM. I'm going to give you a period of seventy-two hours, starting now, that will end this Sunday at 2:00 PM. During this time, you will see that this supposed killer is arrested, and you'll have obtained an *exclusive* confession."

Sacks' face is dominated by a shark-like smile. There's a sneer on the handsome features of the District Attorney. Specs looks relieved. I'm sure he thought that Sacks might somehow blame him for my story, but now that the blame has definitely shifted to me, a small smile is forming. Sad to say, Sacks has not finished his speech.

"McLain, when you're thrown out of the newspaper business, this old fool is going out the door with you." he said, indicating Ben.

Sacks can beat on me all he wants, but now I'm the one who has reached his limit.

"Just a second. Ben has done nothing wrong. I indicated that I had an okay for the story and with the pressure of a deadline hanging over his head, he never questioned what I gave him. You can't treat a valued employee this way."

"Just a second, Mister Reporter. I own this newspaper and

I can do anything I want. When you're out of here on Sunday, he's out with you."

There comes a time when you won't back up anymore. When, no matter what follows, you've had enough and I've had enough of David V. Sacks.

"Okay, if that's the way you want it. Forget the thousands of local papers and syndicated publications my stories helped sell. Forget everything that's gone before, but let me give you the facts of life. Bobby Mason is a killer. I'll get him and an *exclusive* confession and I'll get it before the Sunday deadline. You have to give me your word that when I do, Ben keeps his job until he retires, no matter what happens."

Sacks pauses before he answers. Specs can no longer hold his tongue.

"Our leader is not required to give his word on ..."

"Shut up, Bornheim!" Sacks' words sting the editor like the lash of a whip. Specs shrinks back against the wall. "McLain, you've got a deal. In fact, I like the idea of betting on a sure thing. There's no way you can make this happen." His eyes bore into mine as though he thinks he has x-ray vision and is looking into another world.

He turns away and gives the others in the room a winning smile.

"I have a beautiful lady waiting to join me in a belated lunch." He nods his head toward his chauffeur. "Come, Joseph, it's time to go. Gentlemen and ladies, good day!"

# CHAPTER FIFTY-FIVE

I join Blondie at the Legal Eagle and both of us just pick at our food. Our mutual depression is a signal to the staff to leave us alone and let us sort out our troubles. Being with the department, Blondie can't see that I can effect the capture of Bobby Mason, let alone get an exclusive confession. Tough she doesn't say it, I think she's already thinking about the forced sale of our home, packing the furniture, changing the children's school, and moving to God knows where.

Afterwards, I go to O'Neill's office. He's in court but his secretary tells me he has sworn out a warrant for the arrest of Bobby Mason on suspicion of murder and it is on the teletype to police headquarters around the USA.

Harry Morse stops me on the stairs and informs me he heard about Sacks' timetable. He wonders if I'm not sorry that I pressed so hard to establish that the abandoned 1940 Ford and the one taken on the now infamous demo ride are connected. I reminded Harry that if I had not pressed this issue, Bobby Mason would have gotten away with what had appeared to be a perfect crime.

Harry remains skeptical that Bobby Mason is really the killer and thinks O'Neill has been forced to swear out a warrant just to cover his tracks, in case, and on a long shot, that I'm right. I couldn't care less about why the warrant was issued. The important thing is that it was issued.

Back at the *Reporter*, I have messages from all the radio stations as well as KPHO-TV wanting to do an interview regarding the sensational story naming Bobby Mason as the killer. I throw all of them into the trash basket. The next thing into the circular file is a note from Specs wanting to know if I have any updates on the case. Specs needn't worry. If I have any "updates," he'll be the first to know, or maybe I'll call David V. Sacks and give him my personal views.

Dinner is a complete bust. We urge the children to eat while we slide the food around on our plates, eating little. They know something is wrong, but what's the good in passing on your troubles to kids when they're still just kids? School is coming to a close and at least the boys are animated as they talk about various events that will mark the end of their terms.

I tell Blondie that while the kids take a shower and get ready for bed, I'll do the dishes. I turn on the radio hoping some music will lift my spirits. In a few seconds, the news comes on. The first item of business is the story of the issuing of a warrant by District Attorney O'Neill for the arrest of Bobby Mason.

I shut it off.

I'm not sure I slept a full hour the entire night. I know Blondie never closed her eyes until after three A.M. and the sleep she did manage was not good as she tossed and turned through the long hours.

# CHAPTER FIFTY-SIX

FRIDAY: IT'S MORE OF THE SAME. LOU STEINBERG CALLS THE paper to let me know he's keeping a sharp eye on the teletype just in case anything might come up about Bobby Mason. I know Lou's working on a half dozen cases, but that's the kind of guy he is, always concerned and caring.

Mrs. Roper calls to let me know that Mrs. Severson collapsed after she heard that Mason was wanted for the murder of her son and is in intensive care at St. Joseph's Hospital. I ask if there was anything I could do. The answer was negative.

I watch Mrs. Williams on television doing an interview with KPHO-TV's news chief, Jack Murphy. She is dressed to the nines. Her makeup is perfect and she looks like a movie star. She's having trouble understanding how anyone as tough as her husband could have been surprised and overpowered by a slender young man like Bobby Mason. I could have told her that "overpowering" had nothing to do with it. It had never been a physical contest. When a .45 is stuck in your back, you have two choices: do what the person with the gun requests, or die. In the majority of cases, you get killed anyway, but the only slim chance you have is to obey. I know that in the movies the hero disarms the bad guy and takes over. Don't try it when it happens unless you want a fast trip to the morgue.

If this was a movie, I would have discovered Bobby Mason hiding out in some cheap motel. I'd have forced my way in and either beat the stuffing out of him or drawn my trusty .38 and finished him off. I love movies, but the action they show you when it comes to dealing with bad guys is ninety-nine percent fiction.

Saturday morning, I find Specs in his office deep in conference with the Chicago hot-shot crime reporter Skull Wright. Skull hasn't been around the courthouse, so I have no beef with him intruding on my beat. As I walk through the door, Specs beams.

"Good morning, McLain. You must have a wrap-up on the Mason case for me."

"No such luck."

Bornheim chuckles and I swear he gives Skull a wink.

"The publisher seems to think you have all the time you need."

"Let's put it this way, Specs, David V. Sacks has no more idea how to cover a story than the fireplug on the corner."

The dark eyes flash behind the horn rimmed glasses.

"My name is not 'Specs.'"

I just walked through the door of his office and already I'm tired of the whole conversation.

"Okay, Mr. Bornheim. I want to do another version of the Mason story to see if I can get some help both on the local and national front, but of course to do this I need your okay"

I know for a fact he winks at Skull as he leans back in his black leather chair. The big smile is almost too much for my stomach to handle at such an early hour.

"McLain, you go right ahead and write your story and when you finish, you take it down to Ben and tell him it's to be front page tomorrow and be sure it gets to the AP wire. If he has any questions just have him call me and I'll give him the official okay."

I go back to my desk and stick some paper in the typewriter. Once I start writing, the world drops away and I have tunnel vision on the subject I'm writing about. The story is an update saying that Bobby Mason has not been found and that somewhere he is moving and eating and sleeping with normal people, but that this man is a cold-blooded killer. The police, the DA, and everyone in law enforcement is asking for help in capturing him before he kills again. The headline is very simple. Big and black.

## "CATCH THIS KILLER"

Under the headline we'll feature the photo of a smiling Bobby Mason followed by my byline and the story.

Ben is sitting at his battered desk in the composing room. For the first time, I notice how tired he looks. Maybe that's because he's depressed? He glances up as I walk over and hand him the copy and photo.

"This is it, Ben, our last shot at reaching out to the people of America for help. I didn't think Specs would okay the story, but if you ask him, he'll tell you it's my ticket out the front door."

Ben takes the materials from me. "I don't know, Gene. I wish I could feel better about things. We're almost out of time. I've been here forty years and I don't know what the missus and I will do without this job."

Standing there in his clean bib overalls Ben looks old, tired and beaten. This job, his wife, and the little flower garden at their small home is Ben's entire world, and with the exception of his wife Debbie, he is standing on the brink of losing everything. I drum up a lot more enthusiasm than I feel when I look him in the eye and say, "The power of the press has never failed me. Somewhere, somehow, there's a reader out there who's going to respond."

I go back upstairs and return calls to all my messages. I check out the situation at headquarters only to find out that the report is the same as before: zero.

I make a call to St. Joseph's to see if there is anything new on Mrs. Severson, but she's still in intensive care.

Much later, as I'm leaving the building, I look through the glass and see Ben watching the presses which are going full speed. The headlines fly by like a thousand black streaks.

### "CATCH THIS KILLER"

# CHAPTER FIFTY-SEVEN

I GOT HOME LATE LAST NIGHT. BLONDIE AND THE KIDS WERE already in bed, but my bride left dinner for me in the oven. She made chicken and noodles, one of my favorites, but I didn't eat a whole lot. After dinner, I rummaged through a cupboard and found a half-empty bottle off of Scotch. I poured two fingers, added water, and went into the living room to sit down and think things over. I must have been tired, because I fell asleep and didn't wake up until after 4:00 AM. Blondie will be waking up in two hours and be busy fixing breakfast. Then she and the children will go to church. I fire up the percolator and soon have coffee. I have a cup, and leave an almost full pot that will be hot and ready for when she comes into the kitchen.

I look at myself in the mirror in the downstairs bathroom. It's not a pretty picture. I'm badly in need of a shave and I'm pretty rumpled. Well, that's the way it is. I have a headache, a bitter taste in my mouth and I feel old and tired.

I pop a couple of aspirin's and have a healthy swig of mouthwash. Then I quietly slip out the door, find my car and make my way down the quiet Sunday morning streets to police headquarters.

As I take the stairs to the squad room, I hear a radio playing a new version of "When The Wind Was Green." I feel like I've turned green. I come face-to-face with the big wall clock that's ticking off the hours and minutes of my career. It's not a pleasant sight.

Someone has made coffee. I take the first cup just as Detective Vail enters looking fresh as the proverbial daisy. He's carrying a big box of doughnuts. He snaps on the old Vail personality, trying to be upbeat.

"Bulldog, we've got to quit meeting like this or we'll become known as the coffee and doughnut twins."

"Jim, just break out one of those sinkers, I don't care what kind and I'll freshen up my coffee. Maybe you'll bring me luck?"

"From what I hear, you could use a break."

Jim sets his coffee cup and the paper plate that's holding a couple of iced spuds on his desk, and takes his seat. I drop into the chair by the side of his desk and stuff part of my dunked doughnut in my mouth. Jim takes a big slug of coffee, then launches into the news he has been wanting to tell me.

"I have something for you for your follow-up story on the old man whose throat was cut. His name is Bertran Shavers and he's from North Carolina. At one time, he was a very prominent guy in his corner of the world. A bank president, he headed a variety of good works and spent a lot of time, energy, and money on civic projects. When his wife of forty odd years died, he gave it all up. He left over eight hundred thousand dollars in a bank account plus three big parcels of land. The only heir is his sister who will be here Tuesday morning to claim the body. You can get all the details from her."

"What's the chance of bringing the killer in?"

"Gene, I know who did it and you know who did it, but Quintero won't finger him. After you briefed us on the shirt episode, we raced out and tried to intercept Largo before he got home. We found him, all right, with part of his gang standing on a street corner. He was stripped to the waist and he laughed in our faces when we asked about the bloody shirt which, of course, was long gone. He got lucky that no blood splashed onto his pants, but someday his luck is going to run out. When that happens, I'm going to nail Largo Sanchez and when I do, he'll have a one way ticket to the gas chamber."

The shrill jangle of the telephone breaks into Vail's discourse.

"Phoenix Police Department, Detective James Vail speaking. Let me grab a pad and pencil and I'll be right back with you."

Jim covers the phone with his hand. "Sit tight, Gene, we may have a lead on Bobby Mason."

Jim pushes his rolling chair over to another desk, picks up a tablet and pencil and slides back to the phone. From that second on, I feel like a greased snake on a hot griddle trying to make sense out of Jim's side of the conversation.

"Ok, I'm with you. I'm Detective Lieutenant James H. Vail, Phoenix Police Department, Badge 961. Yes, sir, you are correct. Our District Attorney, William O'Neill, has issued a warrant for the arrest of Robert P. Mason, Jr. known as Bobby Mason, on a charge of two counts of Murder One. Mr. Mason is a law student at Arizona State College in Tempe, Arizona. Tempe is a suburb of Phoenix. We have the information regarding Bobby Mason on the national teletype. You haven't seen the teletype but you're acting on a local tip, is that correct? The person who gave you the tip is a Mister Edward Yarid, that's Y-A-R-I-D, okay, of Lewisburg, West Virginia. That's southern West Virginia, Greenbrier County. How did Mr. Yarid know we were looking for Bobby Mason? You're telling me he learned about Mason from a syndicated story he read in the *Charleston Daily Mail* that was written by Gene McLain of the *Arizona Reporter*. I have it. Thank you, Captain Kishpaugh. Would you please call me at this number as soon as possible after the arrest has been made? Thank you. Thank you very much."

Jim hangs up the phone and turns to me with the notes in hand. "Bulldog, your Irish luck may be working. A man named Edward Yarid read your story in a regional paper this morning. He took a good look at the photo and notified the West Virginia State Police that he thinks Bobby Mason is staying in his home."

"Jim, I don't believe it."

"Believe it. Here's the phone number of Edward Yarid in Lewisburg, West Virginia. You'd better call him and check the story."

I find a big yellow pad on an empty desk and sit down to place my call. It seems like the phone is ringing forever, but I think the gentleman picks it up on the third or fourth ring. He tells me that yes, his name is Edward Yarid, that he lives in Lewisburg and yes, he has contacted the West Virginia State Police. I tell him I'm the reporter who wrote the story and inform him that I'm at police headquarters in Phoenix, Arizona. I tell him we have had a call from a Captain Lonnie Kishpaugh of the West Virginia State Police.

Mr. Yarid tells me that he owns a bed and breakfast in Lewisburg. Yesterday evening, a good looking young man with curly dark hair registered. He gave his name as Charlie Andrews of Seattle, Washington, and said he would be staying in town at least a couple of days. The young man is driving a new Ford convertible. Apple red with a white top, which is parked in the back of Mr. Yarid's place of business. A little while after checking in, he came downstairs and asked Mr. Yarid to recommend a place where he could get a good home cooked meal. Mr. Yarid's daughter, Joan, works at a place called Food And Friends, right in the heart of town, and Mr. Yarid thought he would like the food they serve.

Charlie Andrews found Food And Friends and in turn found Mr. Yarid's daughter, Joan. Her father described her as a very pretty twenty year-old brunette who works at the restaurant to help pay her tuition to Greenbrier College for Women, which is located just a few blocks from their home.

Charlie waited around until closing time and then walked Miss Yarid home. There was a mutual attraction and before they parted they made a date to go to church this morning. The Yarid family have been members of the Old Stone Presbyterian Church for years and the church, like everything in the little town, is a short distance from the Yarid home. According to Mr. Yarid, Charlie and Joan walked to Church this morning and are, at this moment, a part of the congregation."

I ask Yarid if he knows what state license plates are on the red convertible. The answer is Arizona. Since he has told me that Charlie and Joan have walked to church, I figure the car is still parked behind his building. I tell him I will hold the phone, but ask him to go out back and if the car is unlocked, look between and under the seats to see what he can find.

I give Vail and Detective Steinberg, who has just come into the room, a quick update on what is going on. Then, Yarid is back on the phone to tell me there is nothing under or between the seats, but when he opened the glove box he found a .45 automatic.

Mr. Yarid is becoming more and more distraught as he thinks about the possible danger his daughter might be in. Though I have no idea who Captain Kishpaugh is, I assure the man that the West Virginia State Police will take every precaution to be certain his daughter will not be harmed. I inform him that I will call him back to get all the details, but we have to keep the line clear. We say goodbye. I turn to the detectives, whose number now includes George Grasser.

"Yarid tells me the police are going to arrest Mason when he comes out of church. He's scared to death for his daughter's safety. They evidently live close to the church and he's having a hard time staying put."

Grasser splashes a little water of comfort on the hot coals.

"Don't worry Gene, I'm certain that Captain Kishpaugh and his men will make certain the girl is not in danger."

"All I can say, George, is that I hope you're right. I just wish I was there."

# CHAPTER FIFTY-EIGHT

THERE'S NOTHING HARDER IN THIS WORLD THAN WAITING, AND it's twice as hard when your career is hanging in the balance. In some ways, it seems that the big old hands on the clock are racing by; then, on the other hand, it seems they hardly move.

I call Blondie to tell her that we have a line on Bobby Mason, but no one is home. I try her mother and there's no answer. In desperation, I call the lady who lives next door to her mother and hit the jackpot. She tells me that Blondie and the kids stopped by after church and that she picked up her mother and they were going to a movie.

I eat four more sinkers, which I don't need, and put away three or four cups of coffee. I run out to my car and bring back my tape recorder. I hook it up so we can have a record of any and all conversations regarding the Mason case.

Time keeps going by, then the harsh ring of the phone breaks all of our thoughts. Jim grabs it on the first ring. "Detective James Vail, Phoenix Police Department." It's Captain Kishpaugh of the West Virginia State Police.

I punch on the tape recorder.

From the start, it's obvious that Captain Kishpaugh is a

storyteller and that he is going to tell us what has happened in his own way—and he's not to be hurried.

"Well, gentlemen, this is the way things have gone down. After I talked with you, I called two of my top officers, Lieutenants Phil McLaughlin and Phil Gainer, to report at once wearing civilian clothes. I had just finished my first cup of coffee when they arrived at the office. I called Commander Frank Spicer so he would be aware of what was happening and he issued the orders to move forward and to have a back-up of four uniformed officers with shotguns.

"I briefed my men on Mason and the decision was made to make the arrest as quiet as possible when the services concluded at Old Stone Church. My guys are natives of Greenbrier County and we all know the Yarid family. We know Joan real well since we eat several times a week at Food And Friends.

"When the uniformed officers arrived, they were given orders to work their way up through the church yard using the monuments as cover, and to stay out of sight of the congregation. They were only to act if Mason made a break through the churchyard or started firing. Otherwise, they were to be invisible. Meanwhile, the other officers and I planned to make the arrest. The two Phils and I went to Old Stone in an unmarked car.

"As we walked up to the church the strains of 'Church In The Wildwood' were coming through the open windows. The three of us took various positions and in a couple of minutes the doors opened and the congregation spilled out into the beautiful spring day. Most of our people shake hands with the Pastor, then collect in small groups to talk. Phil Mc Laughlin was the first to spot Joan and her guest as they stopped to shake hands with Pastor McIntosh. As they stepped away, McLaughlin called to Joan, and she invited him to meet Charlie Andrews who was staying at her parents' bed and breakfast. Charlie informed McLaughlin that he would be hanging around Lewisburg for a while, as he thought he and Joan could have some good times.

"McLaughlin mentioned that Phil and I were with him, so he signaled us and we all moved into a little circle that was near our car. Joan introduced me to Charlie and we shook hands. Phil

Gainer was introduced and, as arranged, when he shook Charlie's hand, he pulled him a little bit forward. At that instant, I snapped a cuff on his outstretched wrist, gave him a spin and forced the other arm behind him and finished the cuffing. It went so smoothly that I don't think anyone in the crowd noticed anything.

"We surrounded Charlie and headed for the car. Joan, her eyes wide with terror, grabbed my arm and asked what I was doing. As we put him in the squad car, I told her that she would hear about it soon enough. I asked her to please hurry home because her Dad was very worried about her.

"Here we are at the Lewisburg jail. Notification has been sent to your Chief of Police and to your District Attorney that we have Bobby Mason in custody. Mr. Mason has been offered the opportunity to contact his parents or an attorney, but before he will do any of these things, he wants to speak to Gene McLain, the reporter whose story alerted Mr. Yarid. Since Mr. Mason is an adult, he has the right to make this decision. Do you know where we can reach Mr. McLain?"

"He's right here, Captain. I'll put him on."

"Hello, Captain Kishpaugh. I'm Gene McLain of the *Arizona Reporter.* I'll be happy to speak with Mr. Mason."

The voice on the other end of the line is very forceful, very self assured. "McLain? I can't put it all together. You have tied me to a case I had nothing to do with. You have hounded me all over the United States calling me a killer. My family will sue you and then you'll be exposed for the ruthless, glory-seeking phony you are."

"Bobby, you can call me anything you want, but allow me

to set the record straight. I read your thesis about 'The Five Components of Murder' and it has proved to be an invaluable road map. One by one, I've checked the points off and I have no doubt that the .45 automatic in the glove box of the car that you stole will prove to be the murder weapon. That leaves me with just one unanswered element. Point Number Four in your thesis, the motive. Tell me Bobby, what was the motive?"

The pause is so long, I think the line has gone dead.

"Bobby, are you there? Tell me, what was the motive?"

When he answers, the tone of his voice has changed slightly, but he's still the brilliant legal student. "It's so simple McLain, but then, I wouldn't expect you to understand. You see, I just wanted to commit the perfect murder."

# CHAPTER FIFTY-NINE

I WATCH THE TELEVISION IN A CORNER OF THE COMPOSING room. Specs office is packed with TV, film, radio and print reporters from as if far away as Los Angeles, San Diego, San Francisco, and Seattle. I recognize a stringer from both the *Chicago Tribune* and the *New York Daily News.* Specs needs makeup. He looks like a sick worm and in the background, Skull Wright has the look of someone caught in a vice raid. After the introduction by a staff announcer, David V. Sacks makes a dramatic pause before his cane slashes across the front page of the paper which has been mounted on an office wall. The blazing headlines screams.

### "KILLER CAPTURED - CONFESSES TO REPORTER"

Below are photos of Mason, Kishpaugh, Williams, and Severson.

"Ladies and gentlemen, what can I say? We are so proud of Gene McLain, the finest homicide reporter in the nation. We have always been behind him one hundred percent with all the resources of this great newspaper at his command. No matter how much time is needed to complete a story, McLain has it. I want you to know that there was *never* a sliver of doubt that this was a murder case. I can't begin to tell you how proud I am that our man in the field has brought this diabolical killer to justice."

There is a dramatic pause and I can see Specs start to applaud, then realize he is the only one making noise. He stops mid-clap. The camera moves in and Sacks is ready for the kill.

"McLain is the heart and soul of this great newspaper, now and forever. I'm only sorry he can't be with us today, but he is on a special assignment."

I can only stand so much drivel, so I switch off the set and look at the blessed blank screen. Ben is wiping away some tears.

"You saved me, boy. Me and the missus won't ever be able to tell you how grateful we are."

"Forget about being grateful. Just be glad you're not up in Specs' office listening to David V.'s speech. In reality, Ben, there will be many more great stories before we're through, just wait and see. Right now, I have to get out of here before the meeting upstairs breaks up. After all, didn't the Great Man, David Sacks, say I was on a special assignment?"

# CHAPTER SIXTY

I MAKE A FAST EXIT AND HUSTLE DOWN THE STREET TO THE courthouse. Riding up on the elevator, I get several nice words of congratulations on my story from some employees. At the District Attorney's office, I stick my head in and ask, "Is anybody home?"

Coming from behind a file case is Lee Winters, the Assistant District Attorney. This lady is class with a capital C. A lot of guys around this town talk about her glamour. Okay, she has that too. Long legs, full figure, and classic features. Her beauty is almost startling. Today, she's wearing a black linen designer suit. Around her neck on a silver chain is a beautiful opal swan on a turquoise background. Her dark blond hair falls softly to her shoulders. Her story is one that I'm going to write someday, but I'm going to hold it until the time she becomes the DA or a Judge.

She was in her junior year of college when she met and fell in love with a young man who was struggling to pay his way through law school. This guy was a first class opportunist. They were married and he talked Lee into quitting school so she could work at two jobs to pay his tuition. After he earned his degree, she wanted to finish her education. No, he said she had to stay home, have a child, and be a housewife. They had just become the parents of a beautiful little girl when this jerk met a woman who was wealthy beyond his wildest dreams. He wooed her and after quickly divorcing Lee, married this woman and never paid one penny of child support. Lee put her daughter's life before anything else, but still managed to not only finish her regular college work, but also graduated from law school with honors. In the meantime, the wealthy woman dumped her ex-husband. He went off the deep end and was disbarred and later put a gun in his mouth and ended his and everyone else's misery.

Now in her early forties, this brilliant, beautiful lady is on the threshold of a great career. If O'Neill runs for governor, she will replace him. If he remains in office another year or two, she will go into private practice with all the tools to become a legend as a defense attorney. In time, if she desires, she will be a judge. I just hope that somewhere along the way she finds a wonderful man to share her life. She breaks my train of thought when she speaks.

"Tell me, McLain, will the Assistant District Attorney do?"

"You bet, Lee. You're a whole lot prettier than O'Neill and lots more fun to talk to."

"The DA will be back in a second. He's really keeping me busy getting ready for the State vs Mason on two counts of Murder One."

At that moment, the counselor comes through the door rubbing his hands together, feeling very pleased with himself. "I hope Miss Winters told you that the Mason case is going to be a real piece of cake. Thanks to you, Gene boy, I'm already getting lots of national publicity."

Miss Winters is not as sure as the D.A. that they have this case signed, sealed, and delivered.

"Mr. O'Neill, we have to be aware that the Mason camp is bringing in the finest defense team that money can buy. If they go for an insanity defense, this could become a nightmare. I can tell you one thing, they are not going to roll over and play dead."

"Miss Winters, you're a worrier. With Mason's confession to Gene as a matter of record, I'm going to steamroller his defense. Gene can tell you, all it takes is two good Irishmen working together."

O'Neill's smug little secretary enters and walks to the far wall to switch on the TV.

"Mr. O'Neill, I thought you'd want to see this."

On the screen KPHO television reporter, Jack Murphy, appears in a two shot with Bobby Mason. "Mr. Mason, it has been reported that you made a full confession to homicide reporter, Gene McLain. Do you have any comment?"

The camera moves into Bobby for a close-up. A smile brightens his handsome features and he speaks in a sincere tone.

"Mr. Murphy, this is absurd. First of all, I am a superior law student who intends to practice law when this farce is over. As a student of the law, I would never make such a statement and second, why would I confess to something I didn't do?"

O'Neill snaps the set off. His face is flushed. A smile plays around the luscious lips of Miss Winters and I start for the office door, but being McLain, I have to stop and give the DA a parting shot.

"As you said, Counselor. This case will be a real piece of cake."


The Eagle is packed with the lunchtime crowd as Nat "King" Cole's "Mona Lisa" fills the airwaves. I find my bride in our favorite booth. Her face is wreathed in smiles. She reaches out and takes my hands in hers.

"I'm so proud of you, but sweetheart, never again put your career or our future on the line. The pressure and strain is not worth it."

I take my hands away to take a healthy drink of the tasty shake that Jo Oakes has delivered.

"I'll try, and I mean I'll really try not to get carried away with my search for the truth."

I'm glad she can't see my left hand beneath the table top. My fingers are crossed.

# CHAPTER SIXTY-ONE

A BIG MURDER CASE TAKES OVER THE HEADLINES AND THE front pages for a week, maybe two, then if the killer or killers are not captured right away, it fades to page three or page six. After that it moves to the second section and at last fades away. When the killer or killers are captured the whole process begins again.

Behind the scenes, the attorneys for the state and the attorneys for the defense are working fourteen or fifteen hours, seven days a week. Very few stories are placed about what is going on as they prepare for trial. There were a couple of days when it was indicated that Mason's attorneys would go for an insanity defense. In my opinion, that is the only defense that could keep Mason away from a date with the little green room. Bobby wouldn't hear of it, so his people have started to put together what they can in an uphill attempt to defeat O'Neill and the mountain of evidence the state has to offer.

We're into summer and things are mostly routine. I did have the headlines for a couple of days. I identified a member of the infamous Murder Incorporated who was standing on a street corner decked out in cowboy clothes. This character, who had skipped out on a date with the electric chair in New York, was the funniest looking "dude" cowboy I'd ever seen. I knew there was something about him that I should remember, so I went around the block and there he was still standing, watching the passing parade. This time, the traffic light caught me and bingo, I know who he is. I almost get creamed switching lanes, but I drive the two blocks to the courthouse, where I get Detective Palumbo and a young uniformed cop named Sean Patrick. We go on foot, racing back the two blocks to where the guy is still standing. Joe makes the pinch. Sean gets on the phone and calls for a squad car and alerts the FBI office. I get a great story. This "would be" cowboy, who has killed fourteen or fifteen men, informs me that as soon as he gets out again, "I'm a dead man."

I'll worry when I hear he's on the loose. I think this time the state of New York and the Feds are going to be sure he takes that planned ride on "old Sparky."

Blondie has a couple of mildly interesting cases, but for both of us it has been more or less routine. Now, routine may seem boring to you, but to us that means no extra long hours, or danger and stress. Instead, we can be with the kids, have separate times as friends and lovers, and live what everyone else terms a "normal" life.

At the start of the fall, there's a gang murder down on the south side. It happens about 7:00 AM and nine hours later there is a second gang killing with the same MO. All the cops on the force swear that Largo Sanchez is the trigger man in both cases, but it's the same old story. No witnesses who will testify and no hard evidence to tie Largo to the crimes.

During the sweltering summer months, O'Neill, aided by Lee Winters, the Assistant DA, has pressed for the start of the Mason case. On the first week in September the jury selection starts. Mason has five well-known criminal lawyers and the state answers with its heavy artillery of O'Neill and Lee

Winters along with Don Vermeulen and Ralph Morris, two top flight young lawyers who work for the DA's office. From start to finish, the courtroom will be packed.

I'm beginning to think that every attractive young woman in town comes to the courthouse at least once to try and get a glimpse of Bobby Mason. Believe me, Bobby loves it and plays it to the hilt.

Specs has assigned me to not only cover the trial, but to do a series of sidebar features about various key people involved in both the defense and the prosecution.

I have no choice but to do a rehash of the murders, the difficult time of trying to make the pieces fit, and the capture in West Virginia. Pictures of Mason, Williams, and Severson are in almost daily and the AP wire carries many of the stories. At last, everyone is in place and the trial is ready to start. Well, not everyone is in place. On the second day of September, Mrs. Severson dies in her sleep. The doctors, as always, give a lot of mumbo jumbo as to the cause of death. I think the answer is very simple. The woman died of a broken heart after the death of her only child.

The trial is a three-ring circus with O'Neill as the ringmaster. The state has appointed M.G. "Huck" Huckabay as the judge handling the trial. I don't envy him. O'Neill is using the case as a political stepping stone and the defense has so many twists and turns it seems like it will be impossible to keep things straight. But give him his due, Huck is one of the best men who ever controlled a courtroom and despite all the delaying tactics, he is keeping everything on schedule.

The story of the trial can be told in the headlines that precede my stories:

**"TOP LEGAL TEAM HEADS MASON DEFENSE"**
**"O'NEILL WILL ASK FOR DEATH PENALTY"**
**"MURDER WEAPON FOUND IN MASON'S CAR"**
**"MASON SAYS 'I'M INNOCENT'"**

## "MASON TEAM HINTS AT POLICE FRAME UP"

I can't believe it's the first week in November. There are days that I feel my entire lifetime has been spent in pursuit of, or covering, the trial of Bobby Mason. Bobby and I have had eye contact during the trial and a couple of times he smiled and waved. I guess the wave was for me. Bobby is always oozing charm for some sweet young thing in the audience.

The jury got the case yesterday afternoon and was sequestered at the Westward Ho for the evening. They have been at it all day and pretty soon it's going to be dinner time. Hoagy Carmichael is giving out with "The Old Piano Roll Blues" on a cheap little radio when a uniform cop sticks his head in the press room door to alert everyone that the jury is coming in. We hit the stairs like a pack of wolves, then at last we are in the quiet courtroom. Judge Huckabay makes sure that both the defense and the prosecution teams are in place before he asks the fateful question.

"Have you reached a verdict?"

The foreman, a tall, thin man of fifty in a suit that doesn't fit, answers, "We have, your honor."

"And what is that verdict?"

"We, the jury, find Robert Patrick Mason guilty of two counts of murder in the first degree, punishable by death in the gas chamber."

The courtroom goes wild. O'Neill is waving his clasped hands over his head like he has just won the heavyweight championship of the world, or maybe like he has just been elected governor. Young girls have fainted, others are screaming—"No! No!" or "Free Bobby"—at the top of their lungs. The judge hammers his gavel and orders the bailiffs to clear the courtroom.

At the defense table, the attorneys are shaking their heads

in gloom and giving each other reassuring pats on the back. They are mumbling words about turning the verdict over on appeal. The only spark of life is Bobby Mason, who has a big smile and is trying to comfort his mother who's near collapse.

# CHAPTER SIXTY-TWO

Next morning my headline tells the whole story.

## "MASON TO DIE IN GAS CHAMBER"

A week after Mason was found guilty, Judge Huckabay set the date for his execution. Today, I'm here at the back door of the jail to grab a photo of Bobby as they transport him to death row at the state penitentiary. This transfer was supposed to be secret, but someone leaked the news. There's a mob around the place. Extra uniforms have been called in for crowd control.

At last, the back door opens and a shackled Bobby Mason, surrounded by four big uniformed cops and Detective Steinberg, comes out into the sunlight. Bobby blinks his eyes, then flashes a big smile to the gang of girls who are screaming his name. He raises his cuffed hands to wave as the officers escort him into the van and close the door. They waste no time. The van speeds Bobby on his one-way trip to the state pen. The next ride he takes will be as a corpse. As the crowd breaks up, out of the corner of my eye, I see Largo Sanchez with a couple of punks. He's laughing and I know enough Spanish to be able to know that he is telling the jerks with him that Mason wasn't smart or he would never have been caught.

When I get back to the *Reporter* I find a note to see Specs before I leave. He is almost cordial. He asks me to sit down. I take advantage of his offer since it might not come again in the next hundred years.

"McLain, the Mason case has been big and is big for the paper. I've been thinking. Not right now, but before Christmas, I'd like for you to go down to Florence and have a little heart-to-heart with Mr. Mason. Maybe get some new angles on his story that will give us some powerful features before the execution."

Specs has fooled me this time. I had no plans to see Bobby until the night he chokes to death in the little green room. On the other hand, I still haven't pinned him down for a real motive, so maybe this idea isn't so bad.

"Mr. Editor, I think you may be onto something. I'll check in and see if I can visit Bobby the second week in December."

"Good show, McLain. See if we can't get some more prime mileage out of this case."

In November, I cover two stories that manage to squeeze out three or four days of prime print space but nothing that is going to win any awards. Blondie and I have been Christmas shopping for the kids. I have managed to squirrel away enough cash to buy my wife a very nice necklace with a diamond that will surprise her come Christmas Eve. Of course, I still have a few more payments to make, but the store manager knows me and my credit is good.

I got my car radio fixed, so on the drive down to Florence this beautiful and sunny December day, I have enjoyed every-thing from Bing Crosby's "White Christmas" to Gene Autry's "Rudolph The Red-Nosed Reindeer." I like Christmas. If it works right, it really brings out the best in our fellow man.

I pay my respects to Warden Franks. He tells me that Mr. Mason, as he calls Bobby, has been a delight to the guards, friendly and upbeat. A 6'6'' guard leads me across the sun-baked yard in this old territorial prison to the door that opens into Death Row. From somewhere a trustee's radio is blasting The Weavers big hit, "Tzena, Tzena, Tzena."

The row consists of four cells. At the far end hangs an old, ragged brown Army blanket, kept in place on a wire line by four clothes pins. Behind this blanket is the gas chamber. While the sun is warm outside, it's quite cool in here.

I say hello to Bobby, then grab a stool and sit down outside of his cell. Bobby's the only prisoner on death row at this time. The other three cells are made up, but empty. Bobby strolls over to the bars where I'm sitting and finds himself a place on the end of his bunk.

"You know, McLain, I've spent endless hours thinking about how you put the pieces together, pieces that on the surface had nothing to do with each other. I had constructed the perfect crime and you're the only one who could have solved it. The police would never have figured it out."

He takes a breath and looks around the area.

"In a few weeks, they're going to take me out of this cell, pull that old blanket aside and I'll walk into that little green room, sit down in one of those steel seats, and die. I have a proposition for you. Now, I want you to understand: this means a lot to me. I want you to ask the Governor if you can pull the switch that drops the pellets. Why should some dummy do the job? You're the man who gave the case to the state, signed, sealed, and delivered."

I don't know what he expects my reaction to be, but I give him the straight talk he seems to want.

"I don't have any qualms about granting your request. After all, you didn't have a spark of mercy for those men you killed, but I doubt that the Governor will go along. I'll do what

I can, but I can tell you right now, I won't be able to see the Governor until after Christmas."

"Just give it a try, will you? Hell, they should give a dying man his last request."

He smiles, chuckles, then breaks into a roar of laughter.

"That will be the topper, the real topper."

He has trouble ending the gales of laughter that in time bring tears to his eyes.

"Okay, Bobby—I'll give it a try. You know you're full of surprises. I would have never thought that the law would find you in church."

"That's not so hard to imagine. I had a lovely young lady with me and it seemed a nice thing to do. I thought it was pretty funny. These ministers love to preach about good and evil and I proved that evil can be so close they don't even know it. I bet I gave that parson enough material to preach on for the rest of his life. They'll never forget me in Lewisburg."

# CHAPTER SIXTY-THREE

I DIDN'T SEE BOBBY FOR THE REST OF DECEMBER, BUT I DID hear that his parents came down for Christmas week and spent their time between a grubby little motel room close to the prison and the short visits that were allotted to see their son. Our family had a very nice holiday season. We got to spend a lot of time together, which is unusual this time of the year. Although we are honoring the birthday of Christ, there are no weeks in the calendar as violent as the ones during the Christmas season.

I didn't give Bobby a thought until almost midnight Christmas Eve. After the kids were off to bed, Blondie and I played Santa and Mrs. Claus, getting the presents out of hiding and placing them under the tree. It was an up-hill fight getting two bikes assembled, but at last they were done bright and shiny, ready to greet happy young eyes early in the morning. Blondie goes upstairs to get ready for the few hours sleep that are available before the kids wake at the crack of dawn. I walk out on our back patio. The night is cold and clear and the stars are just an arms' length away. From out of nowhere, my thoughts turn to Bobby. Unless a miracle happens, this will be his last Christmas. How strange it must seem to know that his parents are only a few miles away, but he is not now, and will never be, a part of the family again. I wonder if he is thinking of all the happy Christmas Eves he has lived, or does he think about Williams and Severson as he watches the stars through barred windows?

Blondie and I plan to splurge and spend New Year's Eve at The Flame. We'll dance away the old year to the musical blend of Al Overend and his Orchestra. The Mason case has dominated our year and there have been a wide variety of top international stories: The great entertainer Al Jolson died; North Korean forces invaded South Korea and captured Seoul; General Douglas Mac Arthur was appointed commander of the US forces in Korea. In the meantime, the US recognized Vietnam, with the capital at Saigon and sent supplies, arms and military advisors. Ernest Hemingway published "Across The River and Into The Trees," "Cool Jazz" was developed from Be-Bop, and Clifford Odets won the Pulitzer Prize for his novel "The Country Girl." Despite Blondie and I pulling for the film "Sunset Boulevard," "All About Eve" took the Academy Award for best picture.

However, we were right on target when we picked the New York Yankees to win the World Series. The top story for all of s in the USA was the assassination attempt made on the life of President Harry Truman by two Puerto Rican nationalists New Year's Eve is a real winner. Blondie looks so beautiful in her new dress and dancing with her is like being in heaven. As we return home, the phone rings. A man and woman have been murdered, another man seriously wounded, and the killer is holding a woman hostage.

The old year leaves and the new year enters. I'm crouched in gravel and broken glass in an alley holding the hand of a man whose chest is blown wide open by a shotgun blast. He's fighting to stay alive while the bullets from the police and a crazed killer scream over my head. At last, the police get enough tear gas into the house to force the killer out. He is naked with his hands up but at the last second, he reaches behind his back and whips out a .38 that had been taped to his back. He dies in the glare of police-car headlights as twenty or more bullets tear into his body. We get the man whose hand I have been holding and the female hostage, who has been shot by the killer, into an ambulance, but the trip is all in vain. Both die. Add the killer plus the man and woman who started this rampage and the total is five dead. Happy New Year, 1951!

I file my story and arrive home about 5:00 AM. I find my beautiful wife asleep on the couch still wearing her pretty new dress. I cover her with a blanket, then sit down in my easy chair. Her screams at 6:30 bring me wide awake. She is pointing at the front of my shirt, which I had forgotten was covered with blood.

She thought I had been shot and staggered home to die. I assure her I'm fine and we melt in each other's arms, hugging and kissing. Somewhere along the line she whispers in my ear, "Happy New Year, darling."

# CHAPTER SIXTY-FOUR

THE NEW YEAR TAKES OFF WITH A BANG. THE KIDS STAY WITH Grandma, and Blondie and I enjoy five fabulous days near Flagstaff. Some friends loan us the use of their cabin and it's like a trip to another world. The mountain peaks seem to touch the sky and three of the five days we have a beautiful snowfall. Here we're in this cozy pine-paneled cabin with lots of wood cut for the fireplace, no phones, no radios, just the two of us and the beauty of the woods.

I think all couples should find a week each year when they get away from family, from job pressures, from the cares of the world. Maybe you like the seashore, or a trip to a major city, or maybe hiking and camping out. Whatever your fancy, take the time for yourselves. You rediscover the magic that brought the two of you together in the first place. Call it an extension of your honeymoon, a retreat, whatever title you put on it. Just do it. You'll find a glow that will last long after the getaway time is over.

See—I always said that the Irish are romantic.

We get back to everyday life to find that we have really missed nothing. The pressures and the stresses were waiting, and I'm loaded with assignments, including the hearings on the Bobby Mason case. I sent a written note to the Governor, but haven't heard one word in reply. In the meantime, moves and counter-moves regarding the case go on into the spring. Once again my headlines tell the story.

**"MASON EXECUTION SET FOR MARCH 17"**
**"MASON GETS AUTOMATIC REPRIEVE"**
**"O'NEILL SAYS MASON APPEAL A WASTE OF TIME"**
**"MASON CASE TO STATE COURT"**
**"MASON SEEKS LENIENCY FROM THE GOVERNOR"**
**"O'NEILL SAYS MASON SHOULD PAY FOR HIS CRIMES"**
**"MASON CASE TO U.S.SUPREME COURT"**
**"U.S.SUPREME COURT REJECTS MASON'S APPEAL"**
**"MASON DIES OCTOBER 7"**
**"MASON FAMILY TO MAKE FINAL VISIT"**

I'm in O'Neill's office with the team that handled the prosecution. We're waiting for the evening news on KPHO-TV. The screen goes black, then the picture comes up out of focus on a pair of horn-rimmed glasses. News Reporter Jack Murphy picks up the glasses and as he puts them on, the picture becomes crystal clear.

Jack hits his normal lead-in.

"Let's get in focus with today's news. Here in Arizona, the Bobby Mason case that has seemed to have gone on for a small piece of eternity will be coming to its grim ending tomorrow night."

A film clip comes up showing Mr. and Mrs. Mason. Mrs.

Mason is in the arms of a trained nurse as they're leaving the Arizona State Prison. Murphy picks up the dialogue.

"This was the scene at Arizona State Prison late this afternoon after Mr. and Mrs. Robert P. Mason, Sr. of Seattle, Washington paid a final visit to their son, convicted killer Bobby Mason, who is scheduled to die tomorrow night. Mason's only hope of escaping the gas chamber would be a reprieve by the Governor who turned down a formal appeal by Mason's legal team earlier. Mrs. Mason, who is near collapse, hopes the Governor will listen to a mother's plea and save the life of her only son. An interesting sidelight is that the family visit was scheduled for tomorrow. Bobby Mason asked that the final visit be today, rather than tomorrow, to protect his mother from additional pain."

O'Neill switches off the set and looks at his team. "It's over. At long last, it's really over."

At the *Reporter*, I find a note from the Governor. Bobby's request for me to pull the switch has been denied. I call Warden Franks just as he is leaving and ask him to check with Mason if I can see him prior to the execution tomorrow. The Warden comes back in a minute or so and tells me that Mr. Mason will be delighted. "He says that you have stayed away much too long. Oh, by the way, Gene, he wants you to do him a favor. He'd like for you to bring him a pound of black gourmet jelly beans."

I stop at the candy store and buy a pound of gourmet black jelly beans. On the drive home, the radio stations have canceled their music formats to inform everyone over and over again of Bobby's impending death. A radio reporter has interviewed several girls who say they wish they could rescue Bobby and one who claims she might be a suicide if the state murders Bobby. I shut it off. Have people gone crazy? Bobby Mason is a cold-blooded killer. The fact that he happens to be handsome has nothing to do with it.

I'm glad to be home having dinner with my wife and

family, reading to the kids, tucking them in, and then having some quiet time with my wife. I wish I could tell you I slept like a rock, but I didn't. I keep having the same recurring dream. I see Williams and Severson lying in a ditch with their heads blown away and Mrs. Severson asking me to do something to save her boy.

# CHAPTER SIXTY-FIVE

I PICK UP A COPY OF THE *REPORTER* AND READ MY HEADLINE story as I have my coffee and a sweet roll at The Eagle while the DJ spins the recording of "C'est Si Bon"" by one of my all-time favorite singers, Johnny Desmond. During World War II, I heard a lot of Johnny's vocals with the service band led by the late Glenn Miller. Back then, he was Sergeant Johnny Desmond. Now, he's in the top rank of commercial artists.

The steady rain has been falling since early morning, and by the look of the sky, I'd guess we're in for an all-day session. I work my way out of my raincoat and push it to a corner of the booth. After Jo brings me my order, I spread the paper out. It's wet from the rain blowing around the street corner. I take my first taste of coffee this morning and let the headline sink in.

## "BOBBY MASON DIES TONIGHT"

They have a new picture of Bobby, one that was taken during the trial. It's very good. The handsome face, the dark curly hair and the big smile. I wonder how many people really look at the eyes. There's something behind them, something sinister, something threatening. Certainly someone else must see this. It's evident all the young ladies who are protesting Bobby's execution, as told by words and pictures in Pam Rushman's story on page three, have missed it completely.

Pam writes well. I'm happy to see that Specs is giving her something meaty to work on. She's too talented to be banished to scribbling the doings of the social set.

This also says a lot for Specs. He and I have our differences—I know a great deal of it stems from his wanting to be out on the street, hunting the stories, living the life I do. I know I would never want to be an editor, no matter how much they paid me. I'd go crazy sitting behind a desk seeing other guys doing the things that I would give the world to do.

However, the test of time shows that Specs was just a run of the mill reporter. David V. Sacks, despite all his idiosyncrasies, has had a great eye for talent. When Specs was floundering as a reporter, he saw something in this young man that told him he had the organizational and management ability to run one of the nation's finest newspapers. Sacks was right. Specs is a fine editor. Who knows, if he stays at it long enough, he could become a legend like Jim Richardson in San Diego. I guess part of being an editor is having at least one special cross to bear.

Poor Specs, I'm his cross—the rebel who will not conform. No matter how angry he gets he never forgets it's his 'rebel' who brings in the big stories and who's handling of those stories brings awards and prestige to the paper. I guess you'd say it's a marriage of sorts. I have such a wonderful real marriage that maybe my lot in life is to have a working relationship with my editor that is like the marriages of a lot of other guys. Anyway, I'm glad Specs is extending the leash on Pam. He's not going to be sorry.

. . .

211

This is a day that the clocks run faster than normal. I'm constantly aware that at 10:00 PM this evening the State of Arizona will demand justice and a man will pay with his life for the crimes he has committed. I follow my regular routine. I check in at the police department and follow that with a quick visit to the sheriff's department. I find a new case may be developing that could be a big story.

I stop by to see O'Neill and, instead, find Lee Winters. O'Neill won't be attending the execution. Mr. O'Neill likes to put them in the gas chamber, but he doesn't like to see them die in the gas chamber. However, the DA is giving a luncheon speech to a civic group in which he's going to detail how, from start to finish, he brought the Mason case to a successful conclusion. I'd like to be a fly on the wall and hear that speech, but I have my own words to say to my beautiful wife during our quick lunch at The Eagle.

Blondie's personal investigation of some red flags that have developed from an idle remark may be just the tip of the iceberg of a juvenile case that can trigger events that will have national implications. This could be a blockbuster.

It's impossible for Bobby Mason not to be a part of our lunch-time discussion. I'm going to drive down to the prison around six. I'll have dinner at the little cafe in Florence where I always stop.

The rain seems to be getting heavier and I'll be very late getting home. I watch Blondie, slim and beautiful in her dark blue raincoat, weave through the rain and traffic to the court-house and disappear behind its massive doors. I order another cup of coffee and listen to the radio. The DJ stops talking and I enjoy six minutes of uninterrupted music. Dick Haymes sings a pretty tune titled "Maybe It's Because" and 'The Groaner,' Bing Crosby croons about far away Ireland and a place called "Galway Bay." Someday, ah yes, someday, I'm going to save up enough money so that Blondie and I can take a trip to Ireland. I'd love to find my ancestral home. There's no time to dream of that magic land today. I say so long to Mary O. and Jo, then go through the door out into the falling rain. From somewhere in the back of my mind, I remember that my mother used to tell me that rain was the teardrops of the angels. If that's true, they certainly have reason to be crying today.

At the newspaper, I run into Pam and congratulate her on her story in today's paper. She blushes, then smiles, and thanks me for pushing Specs to give her better assignments. I check my messages and return calls, then stop by Specs' office to let him know that I'm going down to Florence early to spend some time with Bobby Mason before he dies. Since this will be the front page wrap-up of the case, Specs is looking for a cutting-edge story on the hours preceding the execution.

Specs spoke to an aide at the Governor's office who has informed him that it seems everyone who is anyone in the state is trying to get invitations to tonight's party. He hands me my invitation. Just to be certain they didn't do anything different, I open the envelope and read the printing that follows the state seal of Arizona.

## THE STATE OF ARIZONA INVITES YOU TO ATTEND: THE EXECUTION OF ROBERT PATRICK MASON, JR.
### 10:00 PM October 7, 1952
### Arizona State Prison
### Florence, Arizona

The invitation is signed by the Governor, all nice and neat.

I can't help but think about the twists and turns that have brought us to this date. A wave of weariness comes over me. I just wish I could go home and shut out the world and sleep with the sound of the rain on the roof, but that's not possible.

When the name of the game is homicide, you take it all the way to the bitter end.

Looking out the window, it seems that the rain has increased its velocity, so I get into my car and start the trip south. Something is going crazy with my radio. All I'm getting is static. It's just as well. I don't think I'm in the mood for music and certainly not for news which will be giving hourly reports as time draws near for the state to exact the death penalty.

I stop in the little cafe at Florence. This is the place where the visiting press, law-enforcement officers, and interested parties always stop before an execution. The reporters talk about cases from the past that were milestones in their careers and speculate how the star of the upcoming show will handle himself. It's all part of the tradition and you could probably trace it back to the beginning of time.

The place is empty now except for Gus, the manager, plus the cook, the dishwasher and me. I'm early because of my date with Bobby. The others will be coming along in the next hour.

I'm drenched. I stand outside of Bobby's cell and remove my raincoat. This piece of clothing is guaranteed waterproof against anything, including a monsoon, so why do my clothes feel damp? I hang my garment on the bars of an empty cell, grab my stool, and take it to the front of Bobby's lockup.

The other three cells on death row are still empty, but by this time tomorrow, three men who killed a bank guard and a town cop down in the southeast part of the state will take up residence. This will be their home until the time the Governor sends out the invitations for their last night on earth.

The storm is raging outside and flashes of lightning can be seen through the barred windows that are high in Bobby's cell. He's wearing a fresh white shirt, open at the neck, and his sleeves are rolled up a couple of turns. His grey slacks have an immaculate crease and look as though they were just delivered from the cleaners. His feet are encased in soft black slippers. The one thing that has not changed is the smile.

"Gene, you should have been here earlier. Dinner was great. I had fried chicken, mashed potatoes and gravy, and lots of ice cream for dessert. Tell me, did you get things set with the Governor for our little party?"

"Bobby, I tried, but there was no way I could pull it off. The Governor said the Warden has to pull the lever. That's the law and it can't be changed. However, I did get your message and I have here one pound of gourmet black jelly beans."

Bobby's face lights up like a Christmas tree when I hand him the sack and he looks inside. He pops two or three in his mouth.

"McLain, you're a prince. You know I like these even better than I like ice cream, and you know how I like ice cream."

I have to laugh. The ice cream story was slowly growing into a police department legend. They like to tell how many times on the drive back from Lewisburg Bobby had them stop so everyone could eat ice cream. I know Lou Steinberg told me he had put on fifteen pounds during that trip, but really couldn't complain since Bobby had treated seventy-five percent of the time. Right now, the young man is really laying waste to the jelly beans, but that doesn't stop him from talking.

"These are first cabin jelly beans. I can't thank you enough. I want you to know that I am really sorry the Governor spoiled our plans. It would have been a first." Bobby samples a couple more beans, then points to the blanket that hides the entrance to the gas chamber. "You *are* going to be there, aren't you?"

"I'll be there, I promise you." I pause for a second before asking what has been on my mind these many months.

215

"Bobby, there's not too much time left and I just have to know why a good-looking, brilliant young man, with every chance to have a long and successful life, took the road that leads to this place.""You mean, what's a nice boy like me doing in a place like this?" He breaks into a burst of laughter. At last, he stops and after a couple of heartbeats he continues.

"It's really a simple story. I had ambition—a lot of ambition. I wanted to be a big-time lawyer and have lots of money, fast cars, and beautiful women. I wanted the kind of reputation that Percy Foreman, William Fallon, and Jake Erlich enjoy. In short, I wanted to be the best, the very best. I had it made. A wealthy family, beautiful home, first-class clothes, a car, and a loving and caring mother. My father is respected and admired not only by the community but by law enforcement everywhere. He was so proud of me when I was playing football and I led our high-school team to the state championship. He never came to grips with the fact that I turned down several major colleges who had offered football scholarships. Football was just something to do. It was never really important to me. My father's life has always been the law and, being Prosecutor, he often held life and death in his hands. The more I hung around his office, the more I realized that I was so much smarter than the people he tried. He never ran into anyone who could commit the perfect crime. The idea of pulling it off set me on fire."

Bobby is really getting into his story. He's up pacing around his cell. Once in a while he pops in a few jelly beans. I'm not going to do anything to break the spell.

"I could have done it—I could have committed the perfect crime except I have one flaw and that flaw is impatience. All my life, I have never been able to wait for things to happen. When I was a kid, I used to raid the Christmas presents under the tree when I knew the family was asleep. I was careful to re-seal the packages and no one ever suspected. When Christmas morning came, I just acted out my part of being surprised.

The same was true of my crime plans. I couldn't wait—I had to force things. I figured I should get something, some kind of prize, for my efforts. I would never be acclaimed or rate newspaper, radio, or TV space since the crime would be perfect. I liked the design of the new Ford and decided that would be my reward. I purchased the old car and knew I would be in the clear with a forged registration and clean plates.

"I got out on Van Buren Street and started hitchhiking, but I was very selective, only drivers of new Fords would see my thumb. A couple started to pick me up, but the light changed and they went with the flow of traffic. I almost got picked up by a young woman with three children, but again, she was trapped in the flow of traffic and had to move before I could reach her car. I didn't care how many people were in the car that picked me up or if they were men, women, or children. After I got in, we would take a nice drive out in the desert. Then bingo, I'd kill them and that would be the perfect crime. The salesmen were just unlucky. They were at the wrong place at the right time. I was so excited. I couldn't wait. I went into Acme Auto, and although the manager saw me, I'd still have pulled off the perfect crime, except you put the abandoned car and the missing salesmen together."

The door from the yard opens and out of the rain and thunder and lightning comes a grim-faced Warden Franks, three guards, and a very nervous Chaplain. Their slickers are shiny with rain. Franks starts speaking when he is still fifteen feet away.

"Time's up, Gene. Mr. Mason has some business to take care of and you'll have to leave."

As I struggle into my raincoat, Bobby comes to the door of his cell and speaks in a stage whisper.

"McLain, they begged for their lives. The big guy who everybody said was so tough—cried like a baby. The other guy, he begged me not to kill him because of his mother. You should have heard him pray. Mark it down, I'm not going to beg. By the way, McLain, I have no regrets. *No regrets.*"

As he speaks our eyes lock and I can see, somewhere in the back of those sparkling black eyes, something sinister, some-thing evil, something that no one else has ever mentioned and now, they never will.

# CHAPTER SIXTY-SIX

WITH OTHERS AS WITNESS, I ENTER THE DEATH HOUSE. BOBBY has drawn a standing room only crowd. I nod to Detective Grasser who is seated in the front row beside Ralph Morris and Don Vermeulen, the tough young attorneys from the DA's office.

Outside, the elements have let loose in all their fury. Listening to the howling wind and beating rain makes me think I'm somewhere in a small portion of hell. I find a spot against the wall where I will be looking directly into Bobby's face.

The tattered blanket is pulled aside and Warden Franks, the Chaplain, and three guards escort Bobby to the place of death. Bobby has a jaunty air about him, the smile is in place and he acts like he is looking for someone. He has to duck his head to enter the chamber and before his arms are strapped down, he finishes the last of the jelly beans and hands the empty sack to a guard who looks flustered. The doctor in attendance makes sure the stethoscope is firmly taped to Bobby's hairless chest. Then the door to the chamber is closed and locked.

Through the glass portholes of the chamber, Bobby's eyes

search the spectators. The Warden's hand tightens on the lever and the pellets splash into the acid below the seat where Bobby is waiting. The first smell of fresh peaches reaches his nostrils and he sniffs lightly and smiles. Now the wispy smoke starts to rise and Bobby is turning his head, looking, looking. Just before the fumes hide his handsome features, our eyes lock. He has found his target. He smiles, winks, and slowly mouths, *"No regrets .... no regrets."*

Then, he's gone.

Everyone rushes to find their cars and get out of the storm. A flash of lightning reveals a black hearse with Washington plates parked by the door that leads to the death house. In a little while, Bobby's body will be placed inside to take the long drive home.

I stop at Gus's for a cup of coffee and a piece of pie before braving the elements on the sixty-seven mile drive back to Phoenix. I run into an old reporter friend from the San Diego paper. We hit on some old times and I would have liked to have talked longer, but I have a story to file and newspapers don't wait.

# CHAPTER SIXTY-SEVEN

I'M ALONE ON THE FLOOR. THE LAMP ON MY DESK PROVIDES the onlylight in this huge room. I go to work in my two-fingered style. By the time I'm finished, the storm is starting to wane. Just a few drops of rain hit the windows.

Tomorrow, next week, next month, next year, there will be other stories, but I'm not certain that Bobby Mason's eyes won't haunt a lot of my dreams.

Old Ben is waiting for me so the presses can roll. "This is it, Gene. Another hour, it will be on the news stands, and the AP boys will have it in a few minutes."

I rub my hands across my face and realize I need a shave. "It's been a long and eventful haul. I don't know about you, Ben, but I'm tired."

"I know it was extra tough for you, Gene. finding unforgiving evil in a young man with so much promise."

"Ben, I feel for his parents. Good, solid people who did everything they could for him. Well, it's over and Blondie is waiting for me and so are a couple of great kids. Tomorrow we're going to spend the entire day having a picnic in Oak Creek Canyon. Take care, old timer. I'll see you soon."

"So long, Gene. Don't make me wait too long for another big story."

After I clean up a couple of things on my desk, I head down the stairs. Passing the composing room, I see the presses rolling out my final headline of the Bobby Mason case.

## KILLER EXECUTED
## MASON GOES TO GAS CHAMBER LIKE HE WAS GOING TO SUNDAY SCHOOL

I leave the building. The storm is over. The air smells fresh and cool. In the east, a faint glow tells me that soon a new day will break.

# EPILOGUE

BLONDIE LETS ME SLEEP LATE THIS MORNING WHILE SHE MAKES the sandwiches, packs cold chicken, and all the other goodies for our picnic. Jerry and Larry find their fishing poles and get them packed in the car. I'm up now, have a quick bite of breakfast, and like the rest of the family, I'm in a holiday mood. I remember that I didn't get my check and we're going to need some 'whip out' cash. I take my car and run down to the *Reporter*, walk over to the bank, and take care of our financial needs for the trip. I hurry over to my set of wheels only to find Blondie standing by her car, in uniform, with no kids in sight.

"What's with the uniform and where are the kids? I'm ready to picnic."

"The kids are going on a picnic with Mother. The High Sheriff called and he needs me for a special assignment. The way I figure it, you and I have about forty-five minutes."

"Am I hearing right? Forty-five minutes?"

Blondie walks over to my car and leans against the passenger door.

"Come on, a great reporter like you certainly knows how

to make the best use of his time, unless of course, you're too tired."

My bride knows how to light my fire. I put her in the passenger side, walk around and get in behind the wheel, and move the car into the flow of traffic.

"How about that, me tired? Sweetheart, we're just starting to live."

Blondie slides over and puts her head on my shoulder, then leans forward and turns on the radio. I start to tell her it's not working when here comes Bobby C singing our favorite song, *"They Won't Believe."* I think he wrote the lyrics just for us.

They won't believe the dream that's ours, the magic moments, happy hours, the quiet times and the laughter we share.

This jaded world can't understand, I kiss your lips, you hold my hand, when our eyes meet, it's heaven apart.

The long day ends, the night is still, alone at last, you're in my arms, so warm, so close to me. My shoulder holds your sleepy head while rainbows kiss the flower beds, falling leaves or snowflakes in a world locked out.The universe goes spinning on, day and night through endless dawns, it's been that way since Adam and Eve, our private world beyond compare, the dreams for two they'll never share, a love like ours, they won't believe.

---

**FOR HIS WORK IN REPORTING AND SOLVING "COMPONENTS OF MURDER" GENE MCLAIN WAS AWARDED A STORY OF THE YEAR AWARD AND A BIG STORY AWARD**

**MAY 1991**

**WALTER CRONKITE OF CBS NEWS PRESENTED THE FIRST ANNUAL GENE MCLAIN SCHOLARSHIP AWARD FOR "OUTSTANDING WORK AS AN INVESTIGATIVE REPORTER" AT ARIZONA STATE UNIVERSITY**

Dear reader,

We hope you enjoyed reading *Crime Components*. Please take a moment to leave a review, even if it's a short one. Your opinion is important to us.

Discover more books by Rena Winters at https://www. nextchapter.pub/authors/rena-winters

Want to know when one of our books is free or discounted? Join the newsletter at http://eepurl.com/bqqB3H

Best regards,

Rena Winters and the Next Chapter Team

# ABOUT THE AUTHOR

Multi-talented Rena Winters has enjoyed an outstanding career in the entertainment industry as a writer, talent, producer, production executive and as a major TV and Motion Picture executive.

Her writing ability won the coveted Angel Award for the "outstanding family TV special, **"How to Change Your Life,"** which she co-hosted with Robert Stack. She wrote the two hour script (and co-produced) for **"My Little Corner of the World,"** winner of the Freedoms Foundation and American Family Heritage awards.

Feature films include **"The Boys Next Door," "KGB, the Secret War," "Charlie Chan & the Curse of the Dragon Queen"** and **"Avenging Angel."**

Her producing credits include **"The Juliet Prowse Spectacular"** for 20th Century Fox, **"Sinatra - Las Vegas Style"** and **"Peter Marshall - One More Time,"** which produced a best selling soundtrack album.

As Executive Vice President, she headed the entire USA operation for the international entertainment giant, Sepp-Inter, producers of TV Series, TV Specials, Feature Films and all areas of merchandising for their animated entities including **"The Smurfs," "Flipper," "Seabert," "The Snorks"** and **"Foofur"** (all Emmy Award winners) plus **"After School Specials"** for CBS-TV.

Author of the bestselling book **"Smurfs: The Inside**

**Story of the Little Blue Characters**" currently available on Amazon and Kindle and in all book stores.

"**In Lieu of Therapy**," released October, 2015, an inspirational and uplifting easy reading book for busy people. Praised by the President of the American Authors Association as a must read.

Contributing author to an anthology of patriots and heroes, "**I Pledge Allegiance**," sponsored by the Wednesday Warriors Writers group currently on Amazon and Kindle.

Latest book – "**Target One**" A story about how terrorism escalates in America. Winner 2$^{nd}$ Place Best Fiction 2018 by the Public Safety Writers Association.

Rena is a contributing writer to the "**summerlin-ww.blogspot.com**" as a member of the Summerlin Writers and Poets Group. She is also a contributing writer to WTTmagazine@gmail.com. She is a former writer/reporter for "**thenowreport.vegas**," an online newspaper.

In addition, Rena has recently completed writing a children's book featuring two rescue cats. She also has a forthcoming cook book for people who don't have time to cook.

Rena Winters was voted one of the "50 Great Writers You Should Be Reading – 2017 and 2018" by The Authors Show.com.

At the College of Southern Nevada, Rena is an adjunct instructor teaching Creative Writing courses. She makes her home in Las Vegas, Nevada and works in her spare time as an editor and ghostwriter.

Printed in Great Britain
by Amazon

10025935R00135